Soldier to Executive

Applying Army Leadership Principles
to the Corporate World

Blake Repine

Published in Australia in 2020 by Blake Repine

Email: blakerepine@gmail.com

Website: www.soldiertoexecutive.com

© Blake Repine 2020

The moral right of the author has been asserted.

All rights reserved.

No part of this publication may be reproduced, stored in a retrieval system, or transmitted in any form or by any means, electronic, mechanical, photocopying, recording, or otherwise, without prior written permission from the author.

ISBN 9780648841203 (paperback)

 A catalogue record for this book is available from the National Library of Australia

Disclaimer

The author has made every effort to ensure the accuracy of the information within this book was correct at the time of publication. The author does not assume and hereby disclaims any liability to any party for any loss, damage or disruption caused by errors or omissions, whether such errors or omissions result from accident, negligence, or any other cause.

This book is dedicated to my wonderful wife, Shannon. Thank you for your love and support and helping me to be better every day.

Acknowledgements

There were a number of people who provided support and advice throughout the creation of this book. First and foremost, I want to say a big thank you to Judy Gregory who is truly amazing! Without her guidance, advice and support this book would not have been possible. Thank you to Kirsty Ogden from Brisbane Self Publishing Service, who not only introduced me to Judy but also gave incredible guidance to help me navigate through the self-publishing process. Lastly, I'd like to thank Dawn Stephenson for helping with editing and advice in putting this all together.

Contents

Introduction 1

A Leader in Training 4

The NCO Creed – a Creed for All Leaders 11

Always Be Professional 15

Communicate, Communicate, Communicate 28

Invest in Yourself 43

Always Have a Strategy 57

Complacency Kills 75

People First 82

Build Trust and Confidence 104

Ten Top Principles for Leaders 122

About the Author 127

Introduction

Exceptional leaders inspire, motivate, and guide the people who work with them. They provide vision and direction for their team and create an enabling environment that lets everyone get on with their work. They support people to make wise decisions. Truly exceptional leaders lead in a way that encourages others to do their best, gives people confidence in their work and in their capacity to make decisions, and develops future leaders.

This book explains the things I've learned about leadership through my experiences in the military, organisations, and boardrooms. I spent almost 20 years as a soldier in the US Army, moving up through the ranks as a non-commissioned officer. In the years since leaving the Army, I've held a variety of leadership roles within organisations and on boards, particularly in the health sector and local government.

Throughout my career I've worked with a huge variety of leaders – some brilliant, some less so. I've learned from them all. In this book, I pay homage to the best leaders I've met. Everything I've learned about leadership has come from them, and this book is my way of sharing their wisdom.

Why a book?

There's no shortage of information about leadership. You won't have to look too far to find leadership discussed in thousands of books, hundreds of university degrees, and countless training courses, conferences, podcasts, support groups, and articles. Many of these are excellent.

So why am I adding to the general noise about leadership by writing this book?

I've realised that the books and courses I enjoy most are the ones that combine theoretical learning with practical experience. I like to hear about other people's experiences so that I can reflect on what happened to them, and then think about how that might apply to me.

I've also realised that my perspective on leadership becomes increasingly rich as I learn multiple perspectives from different sources. Each book, article, and talk teaches me something new.

In this book, I share some of my experiences and learnings in the hope that you will learn something from them. I don't have all the answers (not by any means), but I do have experiences that might be interesting and helpful to you. This book is like a small piece in the giant jigsaw puzzle of leadership. It's relevant to all types of leadership – including leadership in community organisations and not-for-profits, in work teams, as an organisation's CEO, or as a member of a board.

What is a leader?

In the military, I learned to see leadership as a process of influencing other people to accomplish a mission or task by providing purpose, direction, and motivation.

- **Purpose** is the reason for the mission or task

- **Direction** is the how – the way we're going to do it
- **Motivation** is the desire (or the will) to do it.

This definition is simplified and it won't fit every situation. But it's a definition that I find enormously useful every day. As a leader, it's my job to understand and communicate the purpose, direction, and motivation of the organisation so that everyone understands exactly what they need to do and how it contributes to the overall task.

Being a soldier in the US Army taught me two particularly important lessons – about discipline and about reflection.

- Leadership is like anything else in life: the more disciplined you are in the way you go about it, the better you'll be. The best leader won't be the smartest person in the room, or the one with the most education, or the one with the loudest voice. The best leader will be the person with the most disciplined attitude to developing their skills as a leader. Leadership is a skill, and just like any other skill, the more you focus on it, think about it, and practise it, the better you'll get.

- Reflection is the best way of turning experience into knowledge. In the Army, we reflected on every mission and every activity to learn about what went well and what could be improved. I've carried that approach to reflection with me into my post-Army career. I constantly ask questions, like: Why did it go like it did? What could I have done better? What can I learn for next time?

With discipline and reflection, I believe that everyone can develop their leadership skills.

A Leader in Training

Being in the military gave me the foundation I needed to become a leader. It taught me self-discipline, hard work, and self-reflection.

Why I joined the US Army

In high school, I was your typical American jock. I played football and was captain of the wrestling team. For me, high school was a social event. Even though I did well enough in my classes, I lacked self-discipline. I probably could have secured a scholarship to wrestle or play football at a small college. However, at that time in my life, I just wanted to party and have fun. There was no chance I was disciplined enough to go to college.

Instead of going to college, I followed my family tradition and signed up for the Army. I come from a long line of people who have worked in various capacities in the US military. For me it was an excellent career choice. It gave me an opportunity to grow up, learn the things I needed to learn, and lay the foundations for a successful career – both in the military and beyond.

Transitioning out

I left the US Army in 2013, after serving for over 18 and a half years.

Leaving the Army is confronting. You're forced to find a new career in mid-life, and it can be difficult to know what direction to take. Adjusting to civilian life isn't easy. Like many former soldiers, I wasn't sure what I was qualified to do and whether the skills I had learned would transfer over to something new.

There's a widespread perception that the skills and experiences of soldiers are strictly suited to military or combat environments. Because of this, you often find former soldiers working in defence contracting or in industries like security. Another popular option is government work because veterans get preferential treatment when applying for government jobs.

I believe it's a myth that our skills and experiences have limited application. Much of what I learned in the military translates directly to the workplace – whether in the corporate environment, in education, or in government. Every day, I draw on my Army training and apply practical skills I learned in the military.

I was medically discharged from the Army, due to an injury I received in active service. Even though I'd always known that my Army career would end one day, I felt shaken by being forced to leave, particularly because it arrived sooner than I'd expected. The doctors declared that I was no longer deployable, which was devastating. It was a career ender and I felt useless. I struggled with this for a long time.

There's a certain amount of anxiety from fear of the unknown that comes with leaving the military. It's challenging to go off and get what we used to refer to as a 'real job'.

What happens when soldiers are no longer soldiers?

In the US Army, soldiers are eligible to retire after 20 years of service. That's when we qualify for benefits like a military pension. This means most retiring soldiers are approaching 40 years old, still with many working years ahead of them.

I saw a statistic once that stated fewer than ten percent of people who join the Army ever reach their 20-year retirement. But even ten percent of the original intake is a large group of people retiring. Over the years I'd watched a lot of people reach retirement age, and many of them found it difficult.

The military organises a lot of great programs for soldiers transitioning out of the Army to assist them in finding their new career. They taught us basic skills, like how to write a resume and how to apply for jobs. They gave us time off to attend careers fairs, and they introduced us to recruiters who specialised in placing ex-military personnel.

I found that recruiters were interested in little more than my rank and current job. Recruiters seem to use very simple information to match people to possible jobs, without thinking about their education, interests, or skills. Not once was I asked if I had completed any additional education or about the actual levels of work and responsibility within any of the roles I had held.

Most of the work offered to me was for defence contract work – pretty much what I had been doing in the Army for years, but for private companies. I felt that working for defence contractors would be a step backwards. At best, it would be a sideways move. I was concerned that recruiters adopted a factory mentality that didn't offer me much option for career development. I wanted to develop my leadership potential and move into a role where I could see that career progression would be possible.

I prepared for my new career

I realised reasonably early in my Army career that I needed a long-term strategy to plan for life after the Army. I knew that I wouldn't be able to rely on my physical fitness to keep me employed forever. I also realised, quite early in my career, that I enjoyed planning and strategising. I decided that my long-term goal was to be paid to think rather than being paid to be physically active.

I started college a few years after I joined the Army and spent about ten years completing my first degree – a Bachelor of Multidisciplinary Studies. Then, at the same time as I was transitioning out of the Army, I completed a Master's degree in Management and Leadership. I'd always had a keen interest in leadership, but I understood that I needed some training if I was to turn it into a career.

Not long after I left the Army, I did some further study and completed a Master of Business Administration. I was concerned that my Army training hadn't given me what the corporate world would need in terms of financial understanding, and the MBA filled in the skills gap and gave me exactly that.

Establishing life post-military

Leaving the Army can be frustrating and lonely. That was certainly my experience. The jobs I was offered were not the things I wanted to do, and I felt they didn't match my experience and skill level. I was keen to move into leadership positions, but I needed to establish some credibility first. I felt my goals were not well aligned with the jobs I was being offered.

I recognise that sometimes you have to go backwards in a job before you can move forward. It might make sense to accept a lower-level position in a company if there are good opportunities for advancement. But the jobs I was being offered seemed to be dead-end jobs with no foreseeable promotion.

I met my wife about three years before I left the Army, and our son James was born about fifteen months before I left. My wife Shannon is from Queensland in Australia, so that introduced a new dimension into my post-military options. Not only did I need to decide on a career, we needed to decide where to live. We eventually decided to make a new start in Queensland, where I knew nobody and had no career prospects.

We first arrived in Queensland in early 2013, with me on a visitor's visa and unable to work for the first three months. This was actually a good thing. A friend of mine, who had left several years before me, had advised me to take three to six months off after leaving the Army just to get the 'Army out of my system'. That was good advice. The break gave me time to relax and adjust to civilian life, reflect on my career goals, and learn a bit about the Australian employment system. When my three months was up and my permanent resident visa was approved, I was ready to get back to work.

When I looked for work in Australia, I came up against the stereotypes you'd expect for an ex-Army American. People were concerned that I'd shout or that I'd be hard on discipline. People only need to meet me once to realise that's not my style.

I remember talking to one recruitment agency whose representative said they couldn't work with anyone who didn't have Australian qualifications. I asked whether there's a difference in Australia's profit and loss statements or balance sheets. Of course there's not! But I still had to be ready to deal with those types of concerns.

Finding work in Australia

I got my first job in Australia by volunteering to help a struggling business. This business was based in Central Queensland, and it was suffering in the mining downturn. They were cutting back staff because their training and labour-hire services were no longer in demand, and they were in danger of collapsing.

I offered to help them survive the downturn as a volunteer. The business owner was concerned about not being able to pay me, but I felt that successful volunteering would give me the experience and connections I needed to find a paid position. Volunteering would help me to test my belief that my military skills would be equally applicable in the corporate world. If I was successful, the business owner would become my strongest advocate and help me find a paying position.

My last job in the Army had involved implementing a change project in a human resources centre. I'd developed a reputation as someone who could turn problems around and find ways to move forward. So that's what I set out to do for this mining-industry business.

I helped the business to streamline its administration and improve its training operations. I also helped the owner make some hard decisions, including letting staff go. That was tough. But we were working in an environment where no one would have a job if we didn't take some action, so it was really the only option.

We turned the business around, then built it into something that could be sold. For the owner, the outcome couldn't have been better. He had a viable business that he could sell, setting him up for a successful retirement, and for me it was confirmation that my Army skills transferred well into the Australian corporate environment.

The Army taught me that strategic thinking, self-discipline, careful research, real listening, and good (but hard) conversations are the ingredients needed for successful leadership. My experience in the Central Queensland mining-industry company confirmed that these ingredients translate directly from the battlefield to all types of leadership positions.

The NCO Creed – a Creed for All Leaders

For most of my career in the US Army I was a non-commissioned officer (NCO). I became an NCO when I was promoted to Sergeant in 1998, four years after I joined the Army. When I left the Army in 2013, I had obtained the rank of Sergeant First Class, which is classified as a Senior NCO.

Being promoted into the NCO ranks is a big shift for a soldier. In the lower ranks, you do exactly as you're told – you're paid to do the work, not to think. Being promoted into the NCO ranks means taking on a leadership position and undergoing the required training. You learn how to manage, lead, strategise, and plan.

NCOs are often described as the backbone of the US Army. They're enlisted soldiers with special skills and leadership training who supervise lower ranks and ensure assignments are completed properly. When I was promoted into the NCO ranks, the first thing I did was complete the required leadership course.

NCO training provided me with an insight into leadership that has become ingrained into the way I work. If I'm honest with myself, I was a mediocre soldier throughout my career. I did my job willingly and I think I did it well, but I feel that I didn't have an overly successful military career.

But the Army gave me skills in leadership that are directly relevant to the work I've done ever since. Every day, I draw on the leadership skills I developed through my NCO training and I reflect on experiences I learned from the Army.

Even today, almost a decade after I left the Army, I still recite the NCO Creed. I use it to reflect on my decisions and motivate myself to be a better leader.

The NCO Creed

No one is more professional than I. I am a noncommissioned officer, a leader of Soldiers. As a noncommissioned officer, I realize that I am a member of a time-honored corps, which is known as "The Backbone of the Army." I am proud of the Corps of noncommissioned officers and will at all times conduct myself so as to bring credit upon the Corps, the military service and my country regardless of the situation in which I find myself. I will not use my grade or position to attain pleasure, profit, or personal safety.

Competence is my watchword. My two basic responsibilities will always be uppermost in my mind—accomplishment of my mission and the welfare of my Soldiers. I will strive to remain technically and tactically proficient. I am aware of my role as a noncommissioned officer. I will fulfill my responsibilities inherent in that role. All Soldiers are entitled to outstanding leadership; I will provide that leadership. I know my Soldiers, and I will always place their needs above my own. I will communicate consistently with my Soldiers and never leave them uninformed. I will be fair and impartial when recommending both rewards and punishment.

Officers of my unit will have maximum time to accomplish their duties; they will not have to accomplish mine. I will earn their respect and confidence as well as that of my Soldiers. I will be loyal to those with whom I serve; seniors, peers, and subordinates alike. I will exercise initiative by taking appropriate action in the absence of orders. I will not compromise my integrity, nor my moral courage. I will not forget, nor will I allow my comrades to forget that we are professionals, noncommissioned officers, leaders!

A brief history of the NCO Creed

The NCO Creed is used by the US military to educate and remind NCOs about their responsibilities and authority. It also serves as the code of conduct. Each branch of the military has a slightly different version of the Creed, and it's been rewritten a little over the years. The version I've given in the previous section is the version I learned in 1998.

As I understand it, the US Army was experiencing some turmoil in 1973 as the Vietnam War was coming to an end. During the Vietnam War, many Sergeants had been trained only to do one specific job, and NCOs were no longer seen as well-rounded professionals. The Army overhauled its NCO training system and rewrote the field manual about leadership. The NCO Creed was developed as a way to communicate NCO values to officers during their training. From 1974, it was printed on the inside cover of the textbooks distributed to NCO trainees.

When I started my NCO training in 1998, I was required to memorise the NCO Creed. My course included a 30-day residential program. Every day before breakfast and before dinner, we recited the Creed from memory, in formation. If anyone messed up, we all had to start again. And we had to get it right before we could eat. We learned fast! We also spent a lot of classroom time learning about the Creed and understanding what it meant for our work. We had a manual that explained the Creed in detail, and we were expected to take it seriously.

At first, the NCO Creed was a theoretical exercise, based on classroom conversation. I felt that I knew what it meant, but I hadn't seen it in action. It was only later, when I was faced with difficult decisions, that I truly understood its value. I discovered that I could use the Creed to guide me through an ethical dilemma or if I had to discipline someone I knew well. I also discovered that I could use the Creed to help me reflect on what I'd done and whether things could have been done better.

I've realised since that the NCO training and its focus on the Creed is a bit like doing a university degree. The training gives you theoretical understanding, which can be very helpful. But until you actually have to apply that training in the real world, you don't deeply understand how it works. It's the combination of theoretical training and practical application that develops strong leadership.

Over time, the Creed became my 'source of truth'. It still guides me in decision making. It's the best tool I have for helping me to put aside thoughts about self-benefit when I need to make a tough decision.

When I left the Army and began to develop a civilian career, I realised the NCO Creed translates quite easily to any situation. I like to take out the word 'soldier' and replace it with 'team member' or 'employee'. Most of the time it works. You just need to take out some of the military jargon.

This book is my tribute to the NCO Creed. Everything I've learned about leadership is found within it and it is the foundation on which my leadership principles are built.

Always Be Professional

The NCO Creed says:

No one is more professional than I. ... I am proud of the Corps of noncommissioned officers and will at all times conduct myself so as to bring credit upon the Corps, the military service and my country regardless of the situation in which I find myself. I will not use my grade or position to attain pleasure, profit, or personal safety.

The final paragraph of the Creed says:

I will not compromise my integrity, nor my moral courage.

Be professional

The first paragraph of the NCO Creed reminds me that I can never let my professionalism slip. It matters always. Being professional at work is important, but it's not enough. A good leader is professional always, in all situations, in all encounters.

Leadership is not a job where you clock on and clock off. You're always on show, always 'on'. If you're a leader, your work-self and your private-self must match.

Please don't take this to mean that I'm always working or that I'm some crazy workaholic. Far from it! I like to spend time with my family, and I value my rest. It also doesn't mean that I can't enjoy myself. I'm not always serious and responsible. Yes, I go to social and sports events and local celebrations. Yes, I like to enjoy myself.

But I always remember to be professional and I'm always aware of my surroundings. I aim to always behave in a way that reflects well on me, my position, and my organisation. And this applies no matter where I am and no matter what I'm doing.

I believe that everything a leader does will communicate something about their leadership style. People observe leaders and judge them. And I want to make sure that they're observing the leader I want to be.

Here are some examples that I try to apply in my everyday life – some of which I've learned by making mistakes:

- At social and community events, I know I can enjoy myself, but I always remember that I'm setting an example. Have one or two drinks but no more. Never drink enough to lose control.
- When I find myself in a difficult situation – whether in a shop, on the phone, at home, or in any everyday interaction – I try to remember that professionalism must come first. I never let a situation escalate into a shouting match. I try very hard not to snap back with a personal comment. Even in situations that seem to be clearly unjust, I try to respond with thoughtful professionalism. It's OK for me to communicate my needs or concerns, but I try to do it in a way that shows respect.
- I remain professional on the sports field – whether I'm on the team myself or watching my son from the sidelines. I don't want anyone to ever hear me cursing at a referee or shouting at the opposing team. I don't

want anyone to ever suspect that I'm not playing fair. If I want people to respect me at work, I need to show I deserve their respect.
- When I interact with people in service roles – like the barista who makes my coffee or the waiter who brings my meal – I try to treat that person with the same respect as I treat everyone. I try to remember that I'm not their only customer and I can't possibly know about the stresses and difficulties they're facing. I can't demonstrate respect at work and then be rude or demanding when I go out to dinner.
- I think before I accept invitations to events. I take the time to question whether this is the type of event I want to be seen at and whether attending is the best use of my time.

The summary of these examples is simple: Don't be a jackass. Always stop and think. Always be professional and treat everyone with dignity and respect.

Challenge your professionalism

In the Army we used to say that complacency kills. As soon as you become complacent and treat a situation as business-as-usual, you're putting yourself at risk.

I think this applies to professionalism in the workplace. If you become complacent about your position or about your place in the community, you're running the risk that your professionalism will slip.

Challenge yourself with questions and self-reflection to check that you're always being professional. You could make a habit of asking:
- Am I acting right?
- Am I conducting myself appropriately?

- Am I being seen as I want to be seen?
- Am I being consistent?

If you take regular time for self-reflection, you'll improve the likelihood of maintaining your professionalism.

Lead with integrity

Good leaders lead with integrity. They're honest, moral, and ethical. They have a value system that enhances what they do. Most importantly, they're selfless, leading for the benefit of their people and their organisation, not for themselves.

We've all seen leaders who accept a leadership position for their personal gain. These people make decisions that build their egos or advance their careers. While it is okay to be ambitious and want to achieve high levels in your career, don't do it at a cost to others. To these types of people, the best interests of the organisation come second, behind their own personal agenda. Over the long term, there's a danger this will spiral out of control and become institutional corruption.

Ego-centred leadership can start with little things that individually are no big deal. An ego-centred leader might cut corners on company procedures, violate simple policies, or make decisions that benefit themselves. They might decide that the rules and procedures everyone else needs to follow don't apply to the leader.

But each of these little decisions speaks volumes about the ego-centred leader's mindset and values. They're showing others that it's OK to break the rules once you reach a certain position. Over time, the shortcuts may spread, and team members might start to take unacceptable risks. In the long run, an ego-centred leader may create poor organisational culture, or create an environment where illegal, immoral, or unethical behaviour can flourish.

The NCO Creed's statement – *I will not compromise my integrity, nor my moral courage* – is of the highest importance to me. It tells me that I must demonstrate integrity and moral courage always, both through what I say and through what I do. I need to demonstrate it consistently, carefully, and clearly. Any leader who violates the principle of integrity is running the very real risk of losing their credibility and trust. Unfortunately, once credibility and trust are gone, they're unlikely to ever be returned.

Beware the company share package

One trap to watch for as a leader is that you may be given company shares as part of your remuneration package. While there is nothing wrong with this type of compensation, this has the potential to create a conflict of interest, if maximising share value conflicts with the company's long-term interests.

For any leader, maximising profit and making decisions that improve the share price will clearly be important. But a good leader will never make decisions purely on the basis of share value. Share value is just one aspect of the decision-making process. Challenge yourself to think broadly and reflect on the best global decisions for the organisation. Make sure that share value is just one element of the mix.

Accept responsibility

When you're a leader, everything that happens inside the organisation is ultimately your responsibility. If you're in charge and it happens on your watch, then it's your responsibility. You should be ready to accept responsibility for all decisions and actions, whether you were directly involved or not. If it happened inside your organisation, then you created the environment where it could happen.

When you accept responsibility, it's important that you don't blame your team or expect them to accept the consequences for whatever has happened, particularly if they weren't involved. If it was an honest mistake, your team needs to know that you've got their back and that you'll support them if times get tough. This is particularly important in any public-facing communication. Inside the organisation, you might need to research how your decision was made and what you can learn for the future. But to the outside world, the leader needs to accept responsibility and the team needs to know you've got their best interests at heart.

Develop the characteristics of a leader

Good leaders demonstrate consistent characteristics that help them to achieve credibility and respect. Like all aspects of leadership, these characteristics are things that leaders can learn with self-discipline and practice. For most people these qualities don't come naturally. I believe the most important leadership characteristics include:

- Treat everyone with dignity and respect – I try to treat everyone I meet with the same level of dignity and respect that I would like to receive myself; who they are and what they do are not relevant to the dignity and respect I show. This is pretty much the same principle as the Golden Rule – the idea that you should treat others as you want to be treated yourself.
- Be fair and impartial – I try to be consistent and fair with everyone I meet. When I'm making decisions or addressing conflict between individuals, I challenge myself to remain impartial. This is particularly important if I'm on more friendly terms with one person than another. I need to pay careful attention to ensure that I don't think someone is doing a better

job simply because I know them better. The NCO Creed includes a reminder here. It says *I will be fair and impartial when recommending both rewards and punishment.* This is something that requires deliberate, careful attention. I don't believe that it ever comes naturally and it's easy to fall into the trap of showing favouritism.

- Don't get caught up in the drama. Whatever happens, a good leader should keep a level head and be the voice of reason. Some people get caught up in dramatic events and make things worse by contributing to the sense of stress or crisis. A good leader remains separated from the drama and stays calm at all times.
- Show your vulnerability. Leaders are not perfect and leaders don't have the right answer to every problem. It's OK to show some vulnerability and to show that you're not always confident about making the best decision. You are part of a team, and your team will trust you more if you sometimes show that you're vulnerable and ask for their help.

Can you disrespect your junior?

When I was a very young soldier, someone senior to me told me that it's impossible to disrespect people you outrank. He said that disrespect can only ever go up the hierarchy, never down. So, because I was junior and he was very senior, if I said or did something wrong, then I was being disrespectful. But if he was rude to me, that was fine, because his rank gave him permission to behave that way. He could say or do anything he wanted, and it would never be disrespectful.

That person was a bully. He called us names, yelled at us, and threw things at us. He felt that he had a licence to treat us exactly how he wanted. To a point, he was right. As our leader he did have permission to treat us how he wanted. But to my mind he was disrespectful and, in return, we didn't respect him – even though we didn't dare to show it.

Leaders choose how to behave and leaders choose whether to show respect. I believe that the newest, most junior employee deserves the same level of respect as the CEO. Remember that respect is reciprocal and not automatic.

Don't ask other people to do things you wouldn't do yourself

Leaders shouldn't ask staff to do things they wouldn't feel comfortable doing themselves.

By this, I don't mean that you must be able to do every job inside the business. It makes sense to employ experts to fill skill gaps and do specialist tasks. I also don't mean that you should take your turn working in a support role in every part of the business. You employ people to do things so that you've got the time required to do your own job. You don't need to go and sweep the floors because someone else is being paid to do that job.

But as the leader, you should know enough about every position in the business to be confident that the tasks people are asked to do are reasonable and fair. Even though you may never actually do the task yourself, it's your responsibility to be sure that every task is a task you'd be willing to do if the circumstances were right.

The calm, quiet leader

Imagine your stereotypical military leader. Are you picturing a soldier who yells and shouts at people? Who demands respect through bullying? Who treats everyone like dirt and makes sure everyone knows exactly who is boss?

One of the best Sergeant Majors I ever had the privilege of working with was the calmest, quietest leader I have ever met. I never once heard him raise his voice to anyone, and yet this man commanded the highest level of respect possible. If he asked a staff member to do something, they did it, willingly and without asking questions.

I once asked him about how he learned to lead and how he always remained so calm. His answer was simple. He decided to lead that way. He made a conscious decision to remain calm and dignified because he believed it got the best results. Over time, he developed his skills and learned to stay calm at all times.

This Sergeant Major understood that his position gave him a certain level of authority. But he decided to lead without asserting authority. And he quickly discovered that it was the best way for him to lead. He found his staff:

- responded more positively when authoritativeness was removed
- showed greater commitment to decisions because they felt involved and appreciated
- experienced less stress because they felt they had more control over what they were doing.

I came to recognise his calm, dignified style as one of the trademarks of a true leader. An effective leader creates an environment where people want to do the right thing and feel confident about the contribution they make. This is a direct contrast to a commander, who uses authority to demand respect and action.

Control is an illusion

Leaders only have authority if people allow them to have authority. Any idea that leaders have complete control is an illusion. At any time, people can reject or undermine your authority. They don't have to do anything you say.

'But what about the military?' I hear you say. Don't leaders in the military have complete authority? Particularly those Drill Sergeants in the Army – the ones who shout until they're hoarse?

I had a friend who was a Drill Sergeant and he told me a funny story. Apparently when they're training, Drill Sergeants have to command a tree to do something. They keep yelling and yelling at the tree, trying to get it to take action. And that's where they learn about the illusion of control.

The reality is that even Drill Sergeants only have control when their team gives it to them. Their team members choose to comply and they can change their minds at any time.

People choose to comply for a whole variety of reasons. It might be peer pressure, it might be fear of consequence, it might simply be the least worst option. Just because people comply, that doesn't mean they're being well-led or that people are complying happily.

As a leader, it's worth remembering that your sense of control is an illusion. It will help you to stop and reflect. Why should someone do what you want or what you say? What are the possible objections? Is your request reasonable?

Try not to rest your leadership on the threat of consequences. You never want to hold consequences over someone's head as a way of getting them to act. Instead, create an environment where people are motivated to be involved.

Personal gain leads to poor decisions

I remember a Colonel in the Army who tried to avoid personal danger for himself by hiding behind his position. He decided that he could lead his unit from Kuwait, out of harm's way. He stayed comfortably in Kuwait while his unit entered

Iraq. He sent his people into danger, believing that he could make good decisions from a distance. He couldn't, and he was relieved of his duties.

Decisions based on personal gain are normally not this stark. In one of my roles, I needed to make sure I didn't hide inside my air-conditioned office while sending other staff to do outdoor work in extreme heat. In another role, I noticed the senior executive team getting new IT equipment as part of a digital transformation, when the people who really needed the equipment received something of lesser quality.

When leaders consciously challenge any personal gain they may get from a decision, they're more likely to make decisions that benefit everyone in the organisation. One good example is that new initiatives and new equipment should go to the people who need them most, not to the people who are paid the most.

Leaders eat last

The idea that leaders should eat last has been popularised by motivational author Simon Sinek. But it's an idea that comes from the military, and it's a concept I lived every day for my 18-plus years in the US Army.

In the Army, leaders eat last at every meal. Whatever your rank is, you're not allowed to eat before anyone you outrank. The lowest-ranked soldiers are the ones doing the most physical work, and they need access to best food. If we ever run short of food, then the senior leaders are the ones who can do without. They need it least.

In the military, equipment is treated the same way. The people in the lower ranks have the greatest need for the best, most accurate and most innovative equipment. It's all about giving them the tools they need to be successful.

For me, 'leaders eat last' is a philosophy I carry throughout my work. Leaders receive certain benefits, or concessions, just by being in their position, and it's easy to take those benefits for granted – like being invited to events and conferences, being given small gifts, or having access to the newest equipment. I try hard to share these things fairly across the organisation. I'm not the only person who can represent the organisation at events and conferences. I don't need new equipment or an office renovation ahead of other staff. I try to make sure that the most productive parts of the organisation have the tools they need to work as effectively as possible.

Sharing gifts with the team

I once heard about a senior executive who received several gifts each year from visiting dignitaries and from talking at conferences. All the gifts were small, well under the reportable value mandated by the organisation. But rather than keeping these small gifts for himself, the executive used a lottery system to distribute them to staff.

At the December team meeting every year, he asked each person in his 50-member division to select a number from a hat. Each number matched a gift – ranging from promotional USBs and chocolates through to handmade wall hangings.

The gifts were wrapped, and each person opened their gift in turn. In most cases, the executive took the time to explain where and why he'd received each gift. By sharing these gifts, the executive shared the small benefits he had accrued through the team's work.

Don't expect problems to go away

I don't put things off hoping that they will go away. Not ever! In the Army we often had very short timeframes to put things in place. Things always needed to be done yesterday. I learned to address things when they happen. Then once they're addressed, you have to move on. That situation is in the past. I learned not to hold grudges. You don't hold things over a person's head. You move on, even if it's baby steps.

Since leaving the Army, I have worked with several organisations that use their performance management program to address any issues they're having with an employee. On the surface, this may sound logical. The problem is, within many performance management programs, there's only one formal meeting a year to talk about the employee's performance. I have always taken the stance that performance management happens almost daily, not once a year. At any given time, an employee should know exactly where they stand. When the annual performance management meeting comes around, there should be no surprises.

Annual meetings are useful, but they should be more like a goal setting and career planning session, not just a talk about what's been going well and what's not. Annual meetings are an opportunity to talk about what that person wants to achieve in their career, what the next steps are, and the best path to get there. This approach will help you gain a better understanding of someone's ambitions and motivations. It also helps you to better lead them.

Communicate, Communicate, Communicate

The NCO Creed says:

I will communicate consistently with my soldiers and never leave them uninformed.

Communication is a challenge in all organisations. Misunderstandings are common. It's one of those things that is difficult to get just right. The 'Goldilocks-level' of communication is hard to find – people always complain that there's too much, or too little, or that it's not quite right.

In the Army, we paid most attention to top-down communication. A decision was made at the highest levels, and the communication challenge was to make sure everyone knew about it and understood it.

But within our teams, we recognised that communication is always an interaction – it's circular. When you're working in a team, the conversation always goes back and forth. One person says something, the other person asks questions, and on it goes. Most communication within organisations is not as simple as one person telling others what to do.

Communication is circular

Good communication is about give and take, talking and listening. It's a conversation, where people present their ideas, listen to the response, and then come back with new ideas. It's a place where people can ask questions and check their understanding.

For leaders, this means that you can't just communicate *to* your staff – by making an announcement, sending out a few emails, and issuing a newsletter – and then assume that everything will be OK. It won't be. You have to communicate *with* your staff, and that involves listening.

If you don't listen to what your people say, you can't know whether you've got your message across or whether it's been understood. If you don't accept feedback, you cannot know whether people agree that your suggestion was worthwhile.

Summarise to show understanding

When I was a young soldier, I was taught that any time someone gave me an order I was expected to repeat it back to them. So, if someone senior to me asked me to do something, like deliver a package to another office for example, I would repeat back 'yes sir, I will deliver this package to this person in this office'. By repeating it back, I confirmed that I understood what I needed to do.

This strategy of summarising what you've just heard and repeating it back to the person who said it is something that is simple and can be effective. It's a good way of showing that the message was heard correctly and gives the sender an opportunity to ensure their message will be sent as they intended and can pick up communication mistakes before anything happens.

If the person who is delivering the message only has the task of repeating it, then this form of communication may be okay. However, just repeating a message back to someone does not necessarily mean that it was understood. Also, asking someone to repeat something back to you can come across as condescending or micromanaging. If you want to truly determine whether someone comprehends the messages you are sending, you need to look at their actions. Are their actions reflective of what you are trying to achieve? It not, then you need to look at your messaging and determine whether your messages are effective. Remember, communication is circular. To determine whether your message was understood or not, listen for feedback that shows understanding.

Never leave people uninformed

The NCO Creed clearly states that soldiers should never be left uninformed by their seniors. The same applies in the workplace and in the community. People need to be confident that they are fully informed: that they have access to up-to-date information, that they have access to the full story, and that they know how to find more information if it's needed.

Making sure that people feel fully informed is not as simple as sending out emails and newsletters. In each organisation, leaders should develop a communication program relevant to the specific needs of its people. For example:

- If you're working to improve a toxic or suspicious culture, you'll probably need a lot of face-to-face communication with extensive time for listening.
- If you're working in an organisation that's undergoing a lot of change, you may need to organise special events and activities to provide people with information and support.
- If you're working in an organisation that serves the community (like a hospital), you may need a

- community reference group and you may need a presence at public events.
- If you're working in an organisation that's heavily influenced by stakeholders, you may need a stakeholders' advisory group.

However you choose to communicate, make sure that your people feel listened to and involved. Give them opportunities to contribute, show that you are genuinely listening, then report back showing what you did with the information they provided. The bigger your organisation, the more challenging it's likely to be to communicate consistently and effectively.

Don't overdo email

We all suffer from email overload. Many people don't even open half the emails they receive. If you send someone a long message, chances are they'll just read the first few sentences and then give up. Long emails are an almost guaranteed way of creating confusion.

If something is important, I believe it's best to have a conversation. If it's someone in your office you need to talk to, get up and go to that person's desk. If they're located in another office, then pick up the phone and talk to them directly. I cannot count how many times I've surprised someone by either showing up at their desk or ringing them on their phone to respond to an email they sent. If you talk it through, you'll probably be able to solve the issue straight away or get to a decision more quickly instead of sending emails back and forth to each other. And you'll probably understand each other a whole lot better.

I think that most people rely on email technology too much. Email might be quick to send, but it doesn't allow you to see the person's body language or hear the inflection in their voice. It doesn't let you dig into the subject and make sure you understand. It doesn't make it easy to ask questions. If you have a conversation, you can see the objections and discuss them immediately. With email, the same conversation can stretch out over days or weeks, with little misunderstandings and confusions, all caused because you haven't spoken to each other.

Of course, I'm not saying that you should avoid email. It's probably the most useful communication tool we have right now. Just don't overuse it. And don't use email when a face-to-face conversation would be better.

Get out there and talk to people

The idea of management by walking around is hardly new. I've heard that it's been traced back to executives in companies like Hewlett-Packard in the 1970s, and even earlier in companies like Toyota. It's still one of the best management and leadership tools out there.

If you want to lead people, you need to know them and know what they're doing. And to do that, you need to spend time in the workplace – asking questions and listening. I like to ask general questions and then just sit back and listen. If there's something going on, people will eventually talk about it. Often they'll just be happy to get it off their chest – so just by listening you're doing what's needed. But sometimes they'll bring up something that needs a solution, and talking with them might help to make the solution clear.

A good leader is always listening and should always listen more than they talk. Sometimes you can learn things in the most surprising places. I was at the gym one day when I heard a few people talking about their work at the local hospital. I'm on the board of the health service that manages that hospital, but I didn't know these people and they didn't know me. So, I got talking to them with questions like 'I heard you say you work at the hospital. How do you like it there?'

In my experience, people love to be asked about what they're doing and what they think, and I like giving them an opportunity to share experiences with me. As a board member, it helps me to understand more about the organisation I'm helping to lead. It gives me a deeper understanding and helps to alert me to anything that might need more thorough investigation. In general conversations I rarely learn about specific issues with operational significance. If anything of significance is discussed, I can make sure it's handed over to the right person and followed up properly. But what I always gain is a deep, valuable understanding of how the organisation looks to other people, and I'm convinced that helps me to become a better leader.

I'm not suggesting you should become the undercover boss, hiding inside the organisation to observe how people are working. And I'm certainly not suggesting that you should incite complaint. When it's appropriate, it makes sense to let people know why you're interested in talking to them. A lot of the time people are just happy to talk. Most people are very open and they'll enjoy telling you about their experiences.

Once people know you're on a board, you might find it difficult to stop them from talking to you. Being a member of a hospital board often means that a simple trip to the post office will take me some time as I will get cornered by someone who has a concern. People want to tell me about their experiences at the hospital – both good and bad. Often times the person who corners me just wants to feel as if they have been heard. If appropriate, I can help them understand the appropriate path to take action. But I also need to remember my role. If it's an operational issue being discussed, it's rarely my place to get involved.

Use communication to reduce fear

Many people become fearful and anxious when they don't know what's happening and they don't feel they're in control. This can be worse if their organisation is undergoing change. If they're worried, anxious, and apprehensive about organisational change, then you need to communicate clearly to reduce their fear.

Strategic planning and organisational change can be highly ambiguous. You might decide where the organisation is heading, and you might know the big steps to be achieved along the way. But in most change environments, you'll understand the big picture before you can fill in the details. To start with, you might be communicating about the end goal without providing many clear details for people. For staff, that can create uncertainty and anxiety.

Image as an adult, you're lining up for a roller coaster for the first time in your life. As you get closer to the front of the line, you'll become more and more worked up. What will it be like? Will you enjoy it? Will you feel safe? Most other people seem to be having fun, but you hear plenty of screams. Are they screams of fear? What will happen if you get strapped in and then discover you're terrified?

A good strategic plan isn't all that different from a roller coaster. You can't know in advance what the plan will be like as it's being implemented. You can't work out all the details. Much of the work will be ambiguous, particularly the work in the distant future. But, does that mean you should do nothing? Not for a minute!

As a leader, you can manage people's fear of the unknown by communicating clearly, consistently, and regularly. Make sure your people know what the overall vision looks like. Help them to understand what distant future you're aiming towards. Then communicate the details for the coming months and be honest about things that might change along the way. Let people know you're their partner on the journey to change. Help them to believe you have their interests at heart.

As a leader, your communication job doesn't end when you've told people where you're heading. In most cases, this will simply make them feel anxious. People are used to working with the old system, and you probably haven't given them confidence about the new system yet. You're also unlikely to have explained all the steps in getting from the old to the new. You need to make it your business to show everyone that you're on the journey with them. Explain the changes they'll need to make. Show individuals how and where they'll fit into the new system. If training is needed, offer it. The more they learn and the more you communicate, the less anxiety your people will experience.

One of the hardest parts about communicating a new strategy is that strategies, by definition, operate at the strategic level of the organisation. It's not always clear what a strategy will mean for people's jobs. It's your job to create connections between the strategy and the operational tasks needed to accomplish it. People need to understand that their actions will help to achieve the strategic outcome, and they need to recognise their place within it. Try to show each person how the strategic goal links to the job they're doing. Help to ensure they feel a part of the change and involve them in the change process as much as possible. When you communicate clearly, you translate the high-level, strategic change into something that makes sense to people.

Don't take disagreement personally

People are not always going to agree with everything you say. People think differently, have different needs, and have different opinions. Sometimes, they'll disagree with your ideas. As a leader, you need to welcome and encourage disagreement, and treat it with respect.

Disagreement is enormously valuable, if it's handled well. Most of the time when people disagree, they do so because they have the best interests of the organisation at heart. They don't believe the idea being discussed is the best way forward, and they feel strongly enough to talk about it.

The challenge for leaders is to cultivate a culture where people challenge ideas, not individuals. If you can help people to focus on the thing rather than on the person, you're well on the way to achieving a positive outcome.

If someone disagrees with something you've suggested, then as a leader you should welcome it and embrace it. Discuss and challenge the issue, and don't frame it as a personal attack on you. If people disagree with your ideas, take it as a positive sign that they have enough confidence in you as a leader to feel they can question things.

If you encounter negative feedback or disagreement, the worst thing you can do is to shut it down – because shutting it down will create the perception that you're not willing to question whether things could be improved. You're sending a message that it's your way or the highway. If a staff member disagrees once and you shut it down, there's a good chance they'll never feel confident enough to disagree again.

The freedom to ask questions and disagree with ideas isn't something that you can teach down the organisation or something you can tell people to do. You need to demonstrate it yourself consistently, every time. And you need to create an environment where every member of the senior executive team feels confident that they can do it too.

Provide opportunities for questions and challenges

When you're a leader, people tend to go along with what you say. You have authority based on your position, and staff often think they're not in a position to question you.

If you're serious about being an open, effective leader, you need to provide opportunities for questions and challenges. Ask people questions. Watch their nonverbal communication. Dig deeper if you have to.

One approach I use when everyone seems to be willing to agree very quickly is to ask a simple question that takes it away from the individual. I might ask 'if someone did have an objection to this idea, what might that objection be?' Sometimes I might challenge people to deliberately be the devil's advocate – to imagine for a moment that they seriously disagree with everything we're proposing – and to come up with the best arguments against it they can think of. These strategies won't necessarily change our final decision, but they'll open up the discussion and help to ensure we're thinking things through.

Questioning can also work if you present a new idea to people and they don't buy it. Instead of wondering what happened or trying to figure it out for yourself, ask questions. Seek out their objections until you truly understand what's going on.

I've heard that some organisations play decision-making ping pong. They put a net down the middle of the table and sort people into two teams – for and against the idea. The physical barrier of the net helps people to remember what side they're on. Then each time one side puts forward an idea, the opposition counters it. It's a strategy for making better decisions through robust conversation, and for creating buy-in by giving people the space to work through all the objections they can think of. It can also be quite good fun.

Making meetings effective

It's no secret that a lot of work meetings are ineffective. They're often not well planned, don't achieve real outcomes, and do little more than waste people's time. It's only worthwhile going to meetings if you come out feeling you've been informed about something, had some useful discussion, and agreed on some post-meeting actions. Anything else is just a waste of time.

I once worked in an organisation where meetings seemed to drag on endlessly. I was so frustrated that I put together a spreadsheet to calculate the cost of each meeting, with everyone's hourly rate built in. I put it up on the screen in the meeting room, and suddenly we had a money counter instead of a clock. Everyone in the room could see how many thousands of dollars each meeting was costing. Every time a meeting achieved nothing, we could see how much money was wasted.

People in leadership positions are paid for their knowledge and decision-making ability, not for the time they spend sitting in meetings. If a meeting costs thousands of dollars and achieves nothing, then there is no return on investment.

One way I try to make meetings more effective is to restrict the time I'm available. This is an idea I got from a *Harvard Business Review* article: I make a habit of offering half the time people ask for. If someone calls my assistant and asks to meet for 30 minutes, she'll say she can slot them in for 15 minutes. If they ask for an hour, she'll offer half an hour. More often than not, this strategy works well. It helps to focus people's attention on what we really need to talk about. The people who meet with me are more likely to plan for the meeting in advance and more likely to quickly get to the point.

I don't limit other people's time because I don't want to engage with them. I do want do engage, but in a way that's focused and efficient. If you are leading an organisation or if you are one of the main decision-makers, many people will want a piece of your time. You will need to prioritise who gets your time and how much. And some people who want your time are what I call 'time sucks': they suck away your valuable time and waste it. Once you have identified who fits in this category, you can try to limit their time with you and find ways to encourage them to be efficient when you need to meet. Encourage these people to get to the point as quickly as possible.

There's another type of person, the flip side of the 'time suck', who will be your 'movers' – people who are effective, have great ideas, and act. Often, these people need your time in order to get your support. If giving the 'movers' more of your time helps them to achieve more, then it makes sense to give them that time. Giving time to 'movers' is beneficial to the organisation and the team.

Communicating your leadership principles

The first thing a new leader wants to do is communicate their leadership principles to everyone in the organisation. They might give talks, send out emails, or even distribute flyers and newsletters that outline the way they work and the culture they want to create.

Communicating your leadership principles to the rest of the organisation is great, but it can only take you so far. People will believe what they see, and most staff will wait for you to demonstrate your leadership style before assessing what you're like.

This is particularly the case if the organisation is suffering from a poor culture or has been on the receiving end of endless change. People may feel they've heard promises before but the promises have never been delivered. They may also be tired of change.

If this is the leadership reality you face, you need to demonstrate your principles through your actions. It's not enough to say what you believe; you need to live it. And you need to be relentlessly consistent, reinforcing your principles until that's the culture you see.

If you see a team member who doesn't uphold the values you promote, you'll need to call them out on it and bring them into line quickly. Every time you reinforce your values, you'll build a stronger organisational culture. And every day you leave the problems unaddressed, you undermine your chances of success.

Beware the covert dissenters

Sometimes people inside the organisation will resent your leadership style or the changes you're trying to make. You might find some people who do whatever they can to undermine you.

Dissenters exist on a spectrum, depending on how overt they are. Overt dissenters are easy to spot. They're loud about their feelings and open about their beliefs. They might cause problems but, because you can see them, you'll be able to deal with them quite easily.

But covert dissenters are more difficult. They tend to build coalitions behind the scenes and may create a toxic environment without you realising what's happening. You need to be particularly wary about covert dissenters who are professional and pleasant in meetings, but who bully their staff or talk negatively behind your back.

If anyone comes forward and tells you about a covert dissenter, you need to take the complaint seriously. Investigate it immediately. I've been in organisations where high performers are left in place even though they're toxic to the organisation. Sometimes senior managers feel the dissenter's skills or productivity are so important they can't be asked to leave. But if you've got a dissenter in the workplace, that person will undermine other staff and create difficulties in the team. You need to solve the problem – either by encouraging that person to change or by moving the person on.

My experience of removing a covert dissenter

I once removed a high-performing, senior manager from an organisation because she was a toxic bully who treated her team poorly. People didn't want to work with her, but few would complain openly because they were concerned about losing their jobs. Previous managers had decided that her high productivity made her too valuable to deal with. They felt the organisation couldn't function without her.

It took me a while to notice the problem, because I didn't work closely with her and the way she interacted with me was different from the way she interacted with her team. But in my day-to-day listening around the organisation, I realised that people actively disliked working with her. When I started to dig into it, other managers told me they'd had complaints in the past but had decided to ignore them because she was so good at her job.

I don't care how good someone is at their job. If they're not treating people right, then they're not good enough. I refuse to put a dollar over someone's welfare.

It took some time, but eventually I was able to move this person on. The result was almost immediate: productivity amongst staff who had previously been part of her team went up by 20 percent. We removed a covert dissenter who was known for high productivity, and in return we achieved improved morale and improved productivity from everyone.

It's short-sighted to focus on the performance of one person at the expense of their team's morale. In our organisation, the dissenter was a higher performer who led by fear and intimidation. People like that might be successful in terms of productivity in the short term, but in the longer-term people will refuse to work with them. You'll start to lose good people, and the people who stay will probably start to work less effectively.

There are two big reasons why you always need to address covert dissenters – hopefully by encouraging them to change, but by removing them if necessary. Firstly, and most importantly, toxic people will undermine your organisational culture and influence staff morale. You can't keep toxic people in the workplace and hope to create a positive, productive working environment. Secondly, it's your responsibility to mitigate risk. If you're aware that you're employing a workplace bully or similar, you open yourself up to potential litigation and organisational reputational risks from staff who have been treated poorly.

Managing people out of the organisation is difficult. No one wants to be the bad guy and no one enjoys having tough conversations. But if you're the leader, you're being paid to do what's best for the organisation. And it's never going to be best for the organisation to leave a toxic person in place.

Invest in Yourself

The NCO Creed says:

Competence is my watchword. ... I will strive to remain technically and tactically proficient.

The Creed reminds me that competence and proficiency are not something I can achieve and forget. I need to constantly improve what I do, build my skills, and stay up to date. I need to invest in myself and make sure I'm operating at the peak of my abilities. Up and coming leaders should seek out responsibility and take on the hard jobs. Leadership is one of those things where you always keep learning.

Leadership can be learned

Leadership is a skill that can be learned through conscious attention, reflection, and practice. It is not an innate ability. The traditional notion that leaders are born, not made, is simply untrue.

Of course, leadership comes to some people more easily than it comes to others. But if you truly want to be a leader, you can study successful leadership, learn from your mistakes, and improve your abilities. It's a long-term, difficult project. You're not going to attend a weekend conference on leadership and become the next Steve Jobs.

Motivation gets you started

We all know that some days we get up and feel hugely motivated, while other days are a struggle. Motivation is a great way to get started on something new. But motivation is difficult to sustain, and it will only get you so far. When you're trying to achieve something that's big enough to be meaningful, motivation won't be enough. Instead, you need momentum and self-discipline.

No matter what you're doing, you're not going to feel motivated every day. Sometimes you won't know why you're not motivated. Sometimes you won't know what's wrong. You might be tired, or sick, or bored, or simply feel lazy. If you truly want to achieve something, you can't rely on motivation. You need to make taking action a part of your life – a normal part of your routine – and you need to keep at it every day, no matter how you feel.

I come across a lot of people who say they'd like to do a particular job one day. But to do that job, they've got to do some training. At first they're all excited and fired up. Motivation is high. Then they do one term of the course and quit because it's all too hard. When I ask whether their goal is still the same, they often say yes: the goal is still there, but this isn't the right time. It won't ever be the right time until they stop living on 'someday island'. Until they quit dreaming and get on with the work, they'll never achieve that goal.

I'm a weightlifter, and I lift weights most mornings. There are plenty of days when I wake up feeling tired and I'd rather not train. But my promise to myself is that I won't make a decision when I first wake up. I get up, get started, and see how I'm going. Most days I quickly discover that I'm feeling better than I realised, and I'm able to train. It's self-discipline that gets me started every day – the ability to do what needs to be done, no matter how hard it might seem. Self-discipline gets me started, then momentum clicks in and keeps me going. Motivation doesn't stay relevant for long.

Seek out responsibility and take risks

If you seek out responsibility and take on the hard jobs, you'll build your skills and credibility and enhance your authority. In a complex organisation, there will always be tasks that people don't know how to address. Instead of pushing these aside and hoping they go away, you can enhance your leadership potential by taking them on.

Sometimes you simply need the courage to start. Yes, complex jobs are likely to be challenging. Ambiguity and complexity can be frightening. But once you take the first step, you'll often discover that you know what to do next. One step at a time, always asking questions and always assessing your progress is all it takes. You don't need to know what the end goal looks like. You don't even need to know how to get the job done. You just need to know what to do next.

Good leaders are willing to take risks and they have the courage needed to get started. They actively seek out challenges and responsibility. When you take on the hard jobs and risk failure, you will learn a lot and develop confidence.

I remember one patrol during my last deployment to Iraq. During this patrol, we went into an area that we knew was unsafe and had a high number of insurgents. We ended up getting into a short fire fight and one of our team was wounded. The situation was quickly brought under control and we were fortunate that it didn't turn out to be worse than it was. Later that evening, one of the more senior people pulled me aside and said that we could not go into dangerous areas and expose ourselves to potential casualties as it would look bad in the media. I was a bit taken aback because, as soldiers, our job was to seek out the enemy. How could we secure these areas and reduce the insurgents' presence if we avoided them? Unfortunately, in combat situations, the level of risk we must accept can mean a loss of life. The senior person who pulled me aside was not willing to accept this risk.

Fortunately, in the corporate environment, the risks are rarely this extreme. However, I do not take my responsibility for risks any less lightly. In the corporate world, we assume responsibility for risks that affect people's livelihood. Every time we make a business decision, people's careers are on the line. It is this career that feeds, clothes, and houses them and their family. While lives may not be directly at risk, the stakes are nearly as high.

Sometimes we must accept a high level of risk in order to achieve our goals. Many people in workplaces can't shoulder these risks, for a variety of reasons. But for leaders, taking risks and taking responsibility for them is part of the job. This doesn't mean that risk-taking is not stressful: it always is. But if you cannot take responsibility for risks, or if you cannot take risks seriously, then you probably are not suited for leadership.

Push yourself beyond your current role

Early in my career, someone suggested that it's a good idea to work two levels above where you are. If you're hoping to be promoted into a leadership position, this is useful advice.

If you focus on and train for the job that's two levels higher, getting promoted up one level will become easier. You'll already be demonstrating your value to the organisation.

By thinking two levels ahead, you'll become more confident in your abilities and more conscious of the value you bring to the organisation. Thinking two levels ahead will also help you to understand what those positions require, assess you skills gap, and prepare yourself ahead of time.

You can't always know what to do

There are plenty of times at work when you know what needs to be achieved but you don't quite know how to get there. The end goal or outcome might be clear, but the journey itself is a mystery.

As a leader, it's your job to make sure these tasks don't get relegated to the 'too hard basket'. You need to make sure that someone takes responsibility for the task, and you need to provide the support necessary to maximise the opportunities for success. If you're asking someone to work on a task that is complicated and unclear, build in plenty of time for reflection, conversation, and review.

I was working as a manager in a large organisation when a legal issue came up. No one knew how to deal with it and no one wanted to handle it. It was volatile and everyone could see that it was going to be difficult. But it had to be solved. The situation was only going to get worse if we ignored it. I put my hand up to take it on – not because I knew what to do, but because I could see that it needed to be solved and I decided I could cope with the challenge. It took some time and I needed to get help from an outside consultant, but eventually I was able to negotiate an outcome. It took over a year. It was a situation that was never going to be favourable for the organisation, so just by negotiating it to a conclusion I'd been able to achieve success.

That experience reinforced my belief that you don't need to know exactly how to achieve a task. You can learn as you go along and you can ask for help if you need it. Since then, I've taken on several things where I haven't had a clue how we'd achieve the end result. But just by working on it, one step at a time, figuring it out as I go along, it's usually possible to get where we need to be.

If you're seeking a leadership position, then take on the hard jobs. You'll learn as you go along, and you'll develop a reputation as someone who is ready to take on a challenge. When you look back, you might be amazed at how much you've accomplished.

Don't pretend to know more than you do

There are times in everyone's career when you get pushed out of your comfort zone and asked to do something new. Maybe it's a new job or a new project. Maybe it's a new technology. For me, it was a familiar job in a new industry. I was employed to lead a change project in an accounting firm, but I'm not an accountant and I've never been hugely confident about my understanding of the accounting industry.

Clearly, I needed to learn about the accounting industry and my specific organisation as quickly as possible. I was also prepared to admit that I didn't know everything. I was candid about it: I explained what skills I brought to the table and asked for their help in learning how to apply my skills to their industry.

Of course, there was some initial suspicion: what would an ex-military non-accountant have to offer? So, I allowed plenty of time to listen and learn. For more than three months, I did nothing but learn. By the time I was ready to implement change, the staff knew me and trusted me, and trusted that I'd learned about their organisation. Due to taking the time to learn, the project ended up being very successful.

Leaders don't need to know everything – that would be impossible. And they don't need to pretend to always have the answers. Instead, leaders need to listen and learn, then take action based on solid information.

Informal learning is just as important as formal learning

As a leader, you'll never stop learning. A lot of learning is informal – it comes through experience and practice, failure and success. Informal learning is the thing that gives you confidence. Formal learning – from things like university degrees, short courses, and conferences – can provide you with the underlying theory to help you understand your informal learning.

Taking the time for formal learning requires effort and self-discipline, particularly if you're trying to study while working full-time. I hear so many people say they'd like to do formal training but they can't find the time. In reality, it's not time they lack. If something's really important, you can always find the time. It's a question of priority, and whether the investment of time now is worth the payoff in the future. We make time for things that are a priority to us.

Formal education is an investment in your future. Completing a degree might take ten years if you do it part-time. But I honestly believe it's a small sacrifice now for the future benefits it brings. Formal education gives you intellectual skills, which bring high value in the workplace and may outlast your physical skills. I knew people in the Army who lost limbs or suffered catastrophic injuries, and it was devastating for them because our work was based on our physical abilities. It made me realise that formal education was the thing I needed to move beyond physical work and to have a secure career beyond the Army.

Education is a personal investment that no one can take away from you. Yes, it's hard. Getting an education involves sacrifice. But it's well worth the effort.

I hadn't been in the Army for many years when I realised that I needed to get a college degree. I made a conscious decision to study because I knew that my Army career would end one day. My first degree was beneficial to my Army career, but not as beneficial as it has been to me since.

Getting a college education as a full-time soldier was tough. I had to take night classes and do courses by correspondence. I was even taking classes while I was deployed in Iraq. I'd be trying to focus on an assignment, only to be interrupted by a rocket attack.

Our days in Iraq were long. We worked a minimum of twelve hours a day, sometimes longer. We were expected to work every day, for the entire year we were deployed. That workload wasn't unusual, it was simply what was expected. And the work was sporadic. Sometimes I'd be on patrol in the middle of the night, and the next afternoon I might be back out on patrol again.

Even in that environment, I managed to do some study. I didn't do much, just one or two classes, but I didn't give up. I was concerned that if I used Iraq as an excuse for taking a break, then I'd never go back and complete the degree.

I spent ten years completing that degree, and the sense of achievement I had at the end was enormous. It felt like an investment in myself and in my future. Even though it seemed hard at the time, looking back it doesn't feel like it was difficult at all.

Formal education is like so many other things in life. It doesn't take a lot of intellect. What it does take is self-discipline.

So far, I've completed three college degrees – my original undergraduate degree, plus a Master of Arts (Management and Leadership) and a Master of Business Administration (MBA). I'm now working towards my Doctor of Business Administration degree, and I'm determined not to stop until it's done.

I didn't expect to do an MBA when I'd already finished a more general Masters degree. But when I arrived in Australia, I realised that I didn't have enough experience in the financial side of business. Even though I'd handled budgets in the military, I didn't have any experience in handling a profit line. So, I went back to university and did an MBA. It was a great experience and it gave me the confidence I needed to move forward with my career.

Invest in your networks

Good networks are enormously helpful – they keep you connected to other people who are doing similar work and they help you stay up to date with thinking about leadership. I focus my networking on three things:

- *Conferences* – professional conferences are perhaps the best way to meet new people and make strong connections. I see conferences as being better for networking than for learning. Conferences can help to increase your visibility if you're looking for new opportunities.
- *Professional associations* – professional associations can introduce you to new networks, expose you to new ideas, and give you access to formal training. Being an accredited member can bring you credibility and increase your visibility if you're looking for a new opportunity.
- *Former staff and colleagues* – I like to keep in touch and on good terms with most people I've worked with

in the past. We can advocate for each other and help each other to succeed.

One of the networking activities I enjoy a lot is offering support and assistance to people – usually without expecting anything in return. I like to put people in touch with someone who can help them. I like to help organisations find the right person for the job. I like to suggest ideas that may contribute to solving a problem. It's not about being pushy or suggesting that I always know what's right. It's a way of adding value and showing that I care.

Networking does not come naturally to me, and it's something that I've had to invest in consciously. I'm a strong introvert, and I'm not at all comfortable about walking into a room and talking to new people. But it's just like anything else in life: the more you invest in it and practise, the easier it becomes. It's worth the effort.

It's OK to move on

A lot of leaders change jobs reasonably frequently. They're employed to go into an organisation, achieve some concrete outcome, and have an impact. Then they move on to the next opportunity.

I read somewhere that most people start to lose their effectiveness after three years in a role. In the Army, three years would be a luxury – most of the time we had only one year to make an impact before being moved on to something new.

When you know that a position isn't long-term, you learn to do a quick assessment and direct your attention to the issues where you can have the most impact. The Army taught me to work quickly, make sure that people were happy, then move on.

In my first job in Australia, when I was volunteering for a mining-industry company, I moved on when the owner was happy with the change we'd implemented. I went with the company owner to a resource-industry expo and got talking to people from a recruitment agency. They weren't sure that the expo would be helpful for them. The only big role they were looking to fill was with an accounting firm, and they didn't expect to find someone suitable at a resources expo. The accounting firm wanted someone to do a strategic plan and change program. That was me! I started work just a few weeks later. For me it was a testament to the power of networking and being ready to move on when the time is right.

There's no such thing as an overnight success

Sometimes a person will burst onto the world stage. They'll gain sudden public attention and appear to be an overnight success. Perhaps they're a sports star or a celebrity, perhaps a political leader or a forward-thinking entrepreneur. But there's no such thing as an overnight success. It's an illusion created by spontaneous international attention.

When you look behind a successful person, you'll just about always discover their success is based on years of hard work. The idea popularised by Malcolm Gladwell, that success can only come after 10,000 hours of practice, seems about right.

In the weight room, I'm conscious that weightlifting success comes from years of work and thousands of repetitions. As a coach, it's my job to get the weightlifter moving correctly and help them become strong. It's also my job to help them get used to being uncomfortable. Weightlifting is an uncomfortable sport. When you're trying to lift a huge weight, perhaps bigger than you've ever lifted before, it's going to be incredibly uncomfortable. Part of the training is learning how that feels so that discomfort starts to feel normal.

It's years and years of training, repeated day after day, with focus and hard work, that leads to success. It's not worth trying to look for a short cut, because in most things short cuts don't exist.

Learn from mistakes

It's interesting that the NCO Creed doesn't refer to the importance of learning from mistakes. For me, learning from mistakes is important, and I slot it under the part of the Creed about being technically and tactically proficient. As a leader, I can only improve my proficiency if I'm willing to learn from my mistakes.

When I reflect on my time in the Army, I'm not sure the training helped me to reflect on my personal mistakes. We used after-action reviews to reflect on our operational success and think about mistakes at the tactical level. But we didn't spend a lot of time on personal reflection. We learned to question tactics, rather than leadership skills and styles. Most of the time, situations were moving so fast that we didn't have a lot of time for personal reflection.

I learned to reflect on mistakes and learn from them through my university studies and from observing the leaders around me. I'd spend a lot of time watching other leaders and thinking about the approaches they used. The best leaders – the ones who motivated me to do my best – would always find the time to talk through things if something hadn't gone well. They might notice that I hadn't reached a goal or succeeded at some task, and they'd want to talk about what happened and what could have been done better.

I started to notice that I learned a lot from leaders who took the time to talk to me and encourage me. I also noticed that leaders who used punishment or blame taught me about what bad leadership looks like. Being punished would only make me feel fearful about making the same mistake in the future.

There's little point in blaming or punishing someone who makes a mistake. Most of the time, people do the best they can. People will make mistakes. We all do. But blaming or punishing them won't help them to learn for next time and won't help to develop their skills. If anything, blame and punishment will simply increase their fear.

Based on what I've learned from good mentors, I try to notice mistakes, talk about them, and work with people to find a solution. It's almost a partnership approach, rather than a leadership directive. I try to use what insight I have to reflect on what happened and find new ways of working. Mistakes are best seen as opportunities for reflection and learning.

Think like a five-year-old

In July 2017, I gave a short TEDx talk in Rockhampton (Central Queensland).

I'm not a natural public speaker and giving a TEDx talk wasn't something that I'd ever considered. Public speaking used to terrify me, but over time I've learned strategies to be successful. When I was asked if I'd like to be involved in the TEDx event, I decided I should give it a go. It was a great opportunity to practise my public speaking.

I decided that I'd like to talk about how to share great ideas. The trouble was that I couldn't figure out what to say. While I was working on it, my son James came over and asked what I was doing. When I explained it to him, he said that it sounded like fun. That got me thinking. I wasn't having much fun at all! This led me to wondering how I could start to be more like my five-year-old son and find the fun in things. That ended up being the subject of my talk: Stop acting like an adult and start thinking like a five-year-old.

I talked about how adults tend to notice differences and conflict that kids don't even see. In a playground, anyone who plays is automatically accepted. The kids don't ask about skin colour, religious beliefs, or politics. If you're there to play, then you get to play. Kids are also pretty good at solving problems, because they don't know what's not possible. I developed a three-step approach to thinking like a five-year-old: (1) Let go of preconceived notions, (2) Be understanding of differences, and (3) Have fun and enjoy. Next time you get upset about something, try thinking like a five-year-old, and everything might just seem easier.

I enjoyed talking that night, and the people in the room seemed to enjoy what I had to say. A few thousand people have watched it since, and they seem to have enjoyed it. It didn't go viral and it wasn't spectacular. But I wasn't heckled, I still had my job, and my family still loved me. It makes me realise that people often say they want to do something but they can't. In a sense they're right. If they say they can't then they'll never try. I'm never going to be a world-leading public speaker, but I'm proud to say that I gave a TEDx talk.

Always Have a Strategy

The NCO Creed doesn't address strategy directly. But to me, these things are relevant:

Competence is my watchword. My two basic responsibilities will always be uppermost in my mind – accomplishment of my mission and the welfare of my Soldiers. … … Officers of my unit will have maximum time to accomplish their duties; they will not have to accomplish mine. … I will exercise initiative by taking appropriate action in the absence of orders.

Put together, these sentences encourage me to operate at the strategic level. They encourage me to step back and think about what the organisation needs (*accomplishment of my mission*) and what my people need (*the welfare of my Soldiers*). They remind me that I need to provide people with the resources, time, and vision needed to do their work, and then I need to trust them to do that work well.

If you fail to plan, you're planning to fail

Organisations need a strategic plan that guides their direction for the medium term. For most organisations, a three-to-five-year timeframe makes sense for strategic planning. Any longer, and you run the risk of the plan becoming redundant before it's implemented. In a fast-changing world, it makes sense to focus on medium-term timeframes.

A strategic plan provides the goals – the end points – that the organisation will work towards. Without a strategic plan, it's just business-as-usual. And when you're faced with competitors and a changing world, that's like planning to fail. If you don't figure out where you're heading and make a conscious effort to get there, then you're probably going nowhere fast.

Most organisations that I've come across have produced a strategic plan – or at least have had some discussion about where they're heading. But many seem to fail when it comes to implementation. Organisations might lose momentum along the way. Or they might encounter challenges that suddenly make the plan seem irrelevant.

What I see most commonly is that organisations don't implement their strategic plan because they don't ever translate it into an operational plan with concrete KPIs (key performance indicators). A strategic plan offers big-picture thinking about vision and direction, but it's not a document that's easy to implement. If it's not translated into clear KPIs and a good accountability structure, it's near impossible for an organisation to stay on track. You end up with everyone having a vague idea of the end goal, but little shared understanding about how to get there.

The devil is in the detail

Yes, you always need to have a strategy. But the big-picture strategy – the strategic plan – is just one in a suite of strategy documents needed to guide the organisation forward. It's the operational plan with its concrete KPIs that you'll refer to most often.

Employees often feel nervous about strategic planning. I think it's because they can see the end goal, but they can't understand what the journey will be like. Often, they can't see whether they've got a role in helping the organisation reach its objectives.

That's why strategic plans need to be translated into something at the operational level, with much more detail. In an operational plan, you can set out the accountability, discipline, and structure of the work ahead.

Operational plans are an opportunity to be honest with staff. It's likely that you won't know exactly how you'll achieve the organisation's longer-term strategic goals. In the operational plan, you set out the first steps designed to take you on the journey and build in opportunities for review. The operational plan is the place to show staff that you don't yet know how the future will be reached.

A good operational plan is based on the strengths and limitations that each team member brings to the project. It enables you to monitor everyone's progress and adjust the plan if needed.

Try mapping the plan

When I studied for my MBA, I learned about the work of Kaplan and Norton who introduced two ideas I use all the time and have learned to tailor to the varying organisations I work with: the balanced scorecard and the strategy map.[1]

- The balanced scorecard helps to show how intangible assets create value in an organisation. It helps organisations to measure performance in four ways

---

1. Kaplan, Robert S and Norton, David P. 2000, 1 September. Having trouble with your strategy? Then map it. *Harvard Business Review*. Available: https://hbr.org/2000/09/having-trouble-with-your-strategy-then-map-it

– financial, customer, internal processes, and learning and growth. A lot of organisations only measure output, and the balanced scorecard is a way of measuring both input and output. It helps organisations understand how things like internal processes and professional development can contribute to performance.

- The strategy map helps to communicate the balanced scorecard by providing clear and detailed descriptions about who does what and how each activity links to the organisation's goals. It's like a map of what needs to be done to achieve the goals in a strategic plan. It shows how everyone's job is linked to the overall objectives and provides a way of showing how people's work can create value for an organisation.

I use the balanced scorecard and the strategy map both for strategic planning and for evaluating an organisation. It helps me to look at every aspect of the organisation – the workforce, the IT, the processes, and the products being produced – and look for inefficiencies. Each time I locate and fix an inefficiency, I can create capacity that can be allocated to some task that adds value to the company. I hunt out inefficiencies that eat away at the bottom line, find ways to remove the inefficiency, and then allocate the spare capacity to creating new value.

An example here might be automation. When you automate a task that doesn't add value – perhaps some type of administrative process – you free up people's time, increase their time capacity, and enable that time capacity to be used for more value-add tasks. So instead of spending time shuffling papers, your staff can spend more time working with clients.

I worked in a consulting firm where very few of the staff managed to achieve their monthly KPIs. Each staff member was given KPIs around invoicing and billable hours, and only about 5 percent ever achieved the mark. My job was to understand why and find a way to improve their success. I used the balance scorecard to understand how value was being created in the organisation, then used the strategy map to help everyone understand what we were trying to achieve. We embarked on an 18-month change process, with a new client-management system that reduced paperwork and simplified things like data checking and compliance. We flipped the KPIs on their head, transforming into an organisation with over 90 percent achievement of KPIs. In the process, we managed to provide a quicker, better service to clients and even reduce clients' bills.

Change processes are always challenging and some staff will feel uncomfortable about what you're trying to achieve. But if you provide a detailed plan, perhaps through a strategy map, and if you communicate clearly about what you're trying to achieve and why, you're more likely to achieve a successful outcome.

Be open to opportunity

Even while you have your eyes on your end goal, it's important to remain flexible and be open to any useful opportunities that come along. You're only going to notice opportunities if you keep your focus wide and stay attuned to what's going on around you.

One way to achieve this is to encourage your team to keep asking 'why'. Why are we doing this task this way? Is this the most efficient way possible? Is it the best way? How will this achieve what we're trying to do? Would it make sense to try this way instead?

If you encourage people to ask questions, and if you ask questions yourself, you'll create an environment where people look for opportunities to make things better. They'll become more proactive, more accepting of change, and more likely to question whether there are better ways of working.

A good leader creates an environment where strong questions can be asked up or asked down. Team members can ask up – asking about why they're doing what they're doing and whether something could be done a different way. And managers should ask down: why are my people doing this? Am I wasting their time? Do these tasks help to achieve our objectives?

Good questions create an environment where people feel they can challenge decisions and look for better ways of working. The best questions create positive change: they help people look for improvements without critiquing the person or the task being done. The best questions come from a positive mindset where people want to do things in a better or more efficient way.

If you create an environment where people feel comfortable about asking questions, you'll find that a huge number of ideas will start to appear. Most people are full of good ideas, if only they're given an opportunity to contribute. You'll also reduce the risk of the team being willing to blindly follow a poor decision because they don't feel empowered to ask questions or challenge their supervisors.

To maintain the environment where staff feel willing to ask questions, you need to be careful about how you respond to the ideas that are put forward. It's not going to be possible or feasible to adopt every idea. But you need to take every idea seriously, explore whether it is possible, and report back to the person who suggested it.

Seize unexpected opportunities for innovation

When I worked for a large accounting firm, we implemented a change project designed to remove most paper from the workflow. As part of this, we looked for ways to improve efficiencies in the ways we handled electronic files. We had a slow system of checking and double-checking, and we didn't want to simply end up with business-as-usual in an electronic environment.

Going paperless transformed our work because suddenly our staff could work from anywhere as long as they had internet connectivity. Instead of hauling out enormous paper files, all the data was stored electronically.

To address our problems with multiple checking and excessive handling of files, we employed a software engineer who wrote three systems that interacted with the electronic filing.

1. The first provided a traffic light system of things that a Senior Partner needed to check. By highlighting the most important and risky things for the Senior Partner to check, the algorithm cut the Senior Partners' assessment time by around 80 percent.
2. The second brought together multiple entities with the same owner, reducing double-handling and cross-checking.
3. The third provided the staff with a way of monitoring their work in progress. We kept finding that staff exceeded the hours budgeted for a job, leading to us requoting clients and invoicing more than the original estimate. This system aligned the staff's timesheets with the job's budget and provided real-time information about how much of the allocated budget had been used. With this information, staff were able to make better use of the time allocated to each file.

We didn't anticipate needing these software solutions when we first started on the change project to make the office paperless. But as we implemented the paperless office and reviewed its progress, we could see potentially solvable issues that the project was failing to address. We took the opportunity to revise our plan and invest more in software support. As a result, we helped staff to meet their KPIs (which had rarely happened in the past), reduced the time required for Senior Partner checking, improved client satisfaction with fewer budget blowouts, and even managed to reduce some of our clients' invoices.

The message here is that an implemented project doesn't need to fully reflect its original plan. The workplace is dynamic, and it makes sense to seize opportunities when they appear. If that means revising your plan or adjusting your budget, then that's OK.

Incremental steps, always focused on the goal

When you've set an organisational goal, you need to keep focused on that goal and work towards achieving it. Often, the end goal will sit in the future, as something to strive towards. It never changes. And each day, the organisation should take a tiny, incremental step in the right direction. Sometimes the immediate task will seem irrelevant or unimportant to the big picture, but it rarely is.

In the Army, we used to train doing ruck (short for rucksack) marches. They suck. There's no other way to describe them. We'd have to carry heavy weights on marches of 20 kilometres or more. When you're faced with ruck marches, you learn very quickly not to focus on the full distance and not to wonder why you're doing it. You just focus on the next tree and get yourself there. Then you breathe deep and focus on the next tree. Then the tree after that. You take little steps, over and over again, and eventually you get to your destination. By focusing just on those little steps – on the next tree – you feel like you're making progress and getting there faster.

The same applies in the weight room. Every time I lift weights, I focus on that day's lifting and that day's goal. I know what my long-term goal is, but each day I only focus on achieving the goal for that day. If I think about the long-term goal, I'll get overwhelmed and start thinking that I'll never make it. I've got notebooks from my last three years of weightlifting, and sometimes I like to look back and see how far I've come. I can lift weights now that seemed impossible three years ago. It's a great way of motivating myself to keep at it.

Those incremental goals are also important at work. As a leader, you can provide the long-term vision and then help people to focus on the short-term, incremental goals that will help them to get there. Focus on the incremental goals and celebrate each one you achieve. Every so often, take some time to reflect on the long-term vision and celebrate the progress you've made towards achieving it. More often than not, your staff will be surprised by how much progress they've made.

Keep checking your progress

When you're working towards an objective, you need to pause regularly to check your progress. You might ask questions like:

- Are we still heading in the right direction?
- Is this direction still appropriate?
- How are we going with this KPI?
- If we're not on track, why is that? Were we unrealistic in our planning?
- Are there any unintended consequences, positive or negative, affecting what we're doing?

- Has something in the internal or external environment changed?

What's the value of research?

Research gives you an opportunity to discover new things. It lets you scan your environment, see what's going on, ask questions, and make interpretations.

By itself, research doesn't create innovation. Instead, it creates discovery. What you choose to do with that discovery will influence whether you introduce an innovation. Innovation comes from putting discovery into action – it's about implementation.

In most cases, organisations can only be open to the great opportunities that innovation can bring if they do two things: firstly, they're open to discovery through research; secondly, they pause to notice that discovery and reflect on how it could be implemented.

As leaders we need to be attentive to discovery and be careful that we don't ignore it. If we focus too tightly on the goal we're trying to achieve, we may fail to notice the opportunities for innovation that emerge from discovery. We need to constantly evaluate and re-evaluate what we know and what we're doing with what we know. I think of this as being flexible enough to grasp opportunities, but solid enough to have a clear direction.

Think about the timing of your strategy

Different industries require different planning horizons. In some industries, it might make sense to have very long-term strategic plans, with distant planning horizons. In these situations, you'll probably need medium-term and short-term plans that sit underneath the long-term plan.

In any industry, it makes sense to have a short-term – of perhaps twelve months – that guides your most immediate work.

A lot of organisations operate on a twelve-month planning cycle. In the final quarter of the cycle, they'll revise the budget and develop the plan for the next twelve months. The new plan should be finalised and approved before the current plan expires.

While this sounds logical in theory, it brings uncertainty in the final quarter of every year and it creates a risk that the new plan won't be completed in time. In place of a standard twelve-month operational plan, I prefer to develop a rolling plan that gets reviewed and updated regularly. A rolling plan means that, on any given day, your staff will know what they're doing for the next twelve months. To achieve this, I use a twelve-to-fifteen-month planning horizon, review the plan every quarter and update to reflect what needs to be accomplished over the next twelve months. If a project is particularly complex, I might review every month instead of every quarter.

I find that a dynamic, rolling plan helps me to re-evaluate constantly and adjust the work as needed. It keeps the organisation nimble and helps us to respond quickly to change.

Don't try to do too much

It's not possible to achieve too many projects in any given timeframe. The definition of 'too many' will be individual to your organisation and your industry.

I've seen organisations try to complete twelve major projects in a four-year planning period. All twelve projects get established at the same time, with staff expected to monitor and report on each. Little work gets done because the staff are spread too thin and the planning horizon is too long.

Chances are, this organisation will get to the end of the four-year period with just one or two projects completed.

Instead of trying to do twelve projects in four years, it would make sense to choose two or three projects and try to complete them (or at least achieve significant milestones) within one year. Staff will be more focused when they're working on fewer projects, and more able to achieve solid outcomes.

Staff productivity and morale will be improved if people are able to focus on a small number of tasks and make clear progress. I always think that three to five different projects are an optimal number of things for people to work on. This is a good number for people to get a sense of accomplishment, see that they're making progress, but still have enough variety in their work. Any more than five and things start to get confused.

In most situations, it makes sense to focus your resources on doing a small number of things and doing them well.

Avoid the push for instant gratification

A lot of times in business, you need to learn to be patient. Shareholders or stakeholders or the board may be seeking rapid change, and that may not be in the organisation's best interests. Remember that it's your job as a leader to put the organisation's interests and your people's interests first. Be wary of the push for instant gratification and immediate, radical change.

In the push to drive rapid change, it's easy to alienate staff. Staff get tired of constant change, particularly if it seems to be change simply for the sake of making change. If you want staff to feel confident and motivated in their work, you need to address change in a way that's thoughtful, reasoned, and incremental. Instead of focusing on change that will raise the share price or lead to new investment, focus on the long-term best interests of the organisation.

Make change but then give it time to settle and be embedded into the business before you move on to the next thing. Don't operate the organisation like someone who has difficulties with attention and flits from one idea to the next. Don't create unnecessary turmoil for your team.

You need to keep up to date with developments in your industry. You need to adopt change to remain competitive. You want to be nimble enough to embrace change when it's needed.

But too much change at once can be counterproductive. You need to place the necessary change within an overall framework of stability and consistency. It's your job as a leader to monitor the organisation's mood and capacity for change, and to act accordingly.

The tactical pause

When a new CEO is appointed to an organisation, the first question on most people's minds is who will get to keep their job. New CEOs are known for restructures and realignments, so most staff are likely to experience some element of fear. It is best practice for a new CEO to take the first ninety days to assess the new organisation and use this assessment to formulate a plan to move the organisation forward. However, there are often things that will need to be addressed much earlier. Or, there may be pressure on the new CEO to make changes quicker. A good board will work with a new CEO and understand their timeframe for making change.

I was once involved in an organisation that employed a new CEO who was very bright and very progressive. This organisation had been stagnant for the last fifteen years or so – going on with business-as-usual with little change and little achievement. When the new CEO arrived, most staff were enthusiastic and ready for change.

Like most new CEOs, this CEO spent the first ninety days getting to know the business and deciding what to do. And then the change started happening. At first it was positive. Staff were motivated, invigorated, and excited about the future. It was change without redundancy, so people felt reasonably secure.

But every year there was more change, and eventually, people just got tired of it. There's only so much change that people can cope with before they lose momentum and need a break.

Thankfully this CEO was experienced enough to see the strain that constant change was causing. He paused the change program for a full year, giving people time to reconsolidate and rejuvenate. In the military, we called this approach a tactical pause, and it was carefully built into our operational program. Like soldiers, staff need time to rest and let things become bedded down. Constant change can be counterproductive.

Figuring out whether your organisation needs a tactical pause takes experience. You need to monitor all staff and gauge their general fatigue. You can help this process by getting out of the senior executive circle and talking to multiple people across the organisation. Find out what they're thinking and how they're feeling. Have conversations with them and show that you're listening. Be present during these conversations. Then use your people's sentiment to guide your decisions.

Self-reflection: the after-action review

Leaders need to take time out from the busyness of everyday work to reflect on their actions and their decisions. If you don't take the time to reflect, you can't learn from your successes and failures.

For me, self-reflection isn't formalised. I don't deliberately put aside a set time each day for reflection. But it is something that I try to do regularly. I challenge myself with questions like:

- What was my approach like in that conversation/meeting?
- What did I learn?
- Why did it go badly (or well)?
- What could I do differently next time?
- If I'd done something differently, would the result likely be different?

I think it's important to reflect on your successes as well as your failures. We're all ready to analyse our failures and beat ourselves up about what went wrong. If you analyse your successes, you can learn from them and try to improve in other areas. If you can figure out what made you successful – whether it was your style, the governance, the budgeting, or the resource management for example – you've got more chance of being able to adopt those successful strategies in the next project.

I've adopted the Army technique of the after-action review and brought it into my civilian life. Every time I'm involved in a work project, we do a formal after-action review. Everyone involved in the project gets together as soon as possible after the project finished and we ask four simple questions:

- What went well?
- What didn't go well?
- What do we sustain for next time?
- What can we improve on?

The team has an informal, open-ended conversation about these questions, and we record the answers in a way that becomes useful for the next project.

An after-action review doesn't need to wait for the end of a project. If you're doing something big, you might need to conduct an after-action review at each gateway. It's a useful way of doing constant evaluation and checking that the project is on track. If it's not working, you might have an option to pull the project when you reach a gateway review.

One person might be critical to your success

In some organisations, you'll find that one person is a central figure who gets followed by others. That person might have a lot of influence, and their support might be critical to your success.

This happened to me when I was leading a change project in one organisation. I was trying to introduce new technology that would replace old paper-based processes. One team leader, who had a lot of influence, seemed highly likely to resist the change. This person had been operating under the old system for a long time and was extremely comfortable with it. There was a good chance that new technology would make this person nervous.

I knew I needed this person on side, so I invited her to become the project champion. The idea was that she and I would meet regularly to discuss the project's progress, and she would then communicate it to her team. She had access to early training and extra information so that she understood exactly what was happening and could help pave the way for smooth implementation. She accepted the project and got excited about it, and her enthusiasm made implementation easy.

I chose this person as a project champion based on my judgement that special involvement and a sense of responsibility would help bring this person on side. Clearly, this could have backfired. Maybe I just got lucky. But it was a decision based on evaluating the organisation and providing this team leader with just the right amount of challenge.

Disruptive strategy

I learned a lot about leadership strategy by studying the work of Clayton Christensen, who coined the term 'disruptive innovation' to describe innovations that create new markets and disrupt old ways of working. I did his course in disruptive strategy through the Harvard Business School. His ideas influenced my thinking a lot and have made an impact on my development as a senior executive. I was sad to hear that Christensen passed away in early 2020. He's a big loss to the business community.

What job is that product doing?

One of Christensen's key ideas is that people buy things because they want the things to do a job in their lives. They're not purchasing a thing so much as they're purchasing an outcome or a meaning. It's the job the product or service does that matters, not the product or service itself. Leaders and marketing specialists often assume they understand why people buy their products or services, but if they don't do good research, they may not be right.

Christensen used McDonald's milk shakes as an example. Milkshake sales weren't as high as McDonald's wanted, and advertising was having little impact. So, McDonald's did some research with milkshake customers to find out why they bought McDonald's milkshakes. If you try to imagine that a milkshake has a job to do, what is it? It turned out that most customers who bought McDonald's milkshakes had a long commute, and they chose the milkshake because it was thick and filling. Knowing this helped McDonald's to tailor its marketing strategy.

Christensen argues that organisations need to get to the root of why people want their product or service. And the best way to do this is to listen to the market.

It's not so different inside an organisation. If you want to understand why something is happening, you need to listen to people and ask questions. At the board level, it's often tempting to see every issue as financial. Board members look at a set of financial statements, look for points of financial pain, and use those points as a basis for decision-making. While this does get to the root of many issues, the problem isn't always financial, and a good leader will ask questions to uncover the cause. It might be a problem with people, or leadership, or efficiency, or creativity and innovation. You can only find out if you're willing to listen.

Just as people will hire (or buy) a product or service to perform a job in their lives, people also hire your company as their employer. We've all heard the saying that people leave managers, not organisations. Always remember that your people have a choice about where they work and it's your job to encourage them to stay. If you value your people, it will be your organisation they'll hire as their employer and you they hire to lead them.

Complacency Kills

The NCO Creed doesn't specifically mention complacency, but the warning against it is there in every part of every sentence. In its entirety, the NCO Creed is a rally cry to avoid complacency in all aspects of the job. That's because every soldier knows the outcome of complacency: complacency kills. In the Army, complacency kills soldiers. In the workplace, complacency kills competitive advantage and strategic direction.

Competitive advantage is temporary

In the Army and in the workplace, any competitive advantage you gain is temporary and easily lost. It's easy to think that your competitors/enemies are not as smart as you or as vigilant as you. It's easy to develop a successful way of working and then to blindly apply it without variation.

But your competitors/enemies are smart and they are vigilant. They're watching how you work, and they'll get clued into your tactics. If you don't vary your tactics sometimes, they'll know exactly how and when to hit you. And it will hurt.

In the Army, we changed our tactics frequently. We'd do something for a while, watch for signs that our enemy was catching on to what we were doing, and then change things up a bit. Sometimes we made the change too late, after our enemy had figured out what we were doing and had found a way to counter it.

It's the same in business. You have competitors out there, and their objective is to be better than you. They're going to watch what you're doing and look for opportunities to be better than you. In turn, you need to watch your competitors and do everything possible to stay out in front.

Maintaining competitive advantage is enormously difficult. A lot of the time, you're not going to realise that your competitor has caught up with you until it's too late. By the time you realise they're catching up, they're already in front. And then it's you playing the catch-up game.

If you remember that your competitive advantage is temporary, you'll be more ready to do the work that's required to keep reaching for new ground. If you're standing still in business, you're falling behind. Even when you discover a particularly brilliant way of working, you can't sit back on your heels. It won't be long before someone else comes up with a better idea that surpasses your way of working. In business, like in the Army, you need to be constantly looking at what you're doing and how you're doing it, and challenging everyone to find ways to do it better.

The search for competitive advantage applies to every part of the business

Ideally, you'll be able to push the search for competitive advantage and workplace efficiency to every part of the organisation. While the search for efficiency is led from the top, you'll want to get everyone involved in finding ways to make it work. In a cooperative and welcoming environment, staff will feel able to question the ways they do things and suggest opportunities for improvement.

I once worked in a large education institution that was nearing the end of a digitisation process designed to reduce paperwork and processing times. One day I was in the printing and publishing department, waiting for the manager to get back to her desk. While I waited, I got chatting to the department's administrator, and I asked why the department had shelf upon shelf of envelopes. It turned out that we were mailing out students' results every time a student completed an assessment, even though we'd just digitised the entire results system. Instead of reducing processes, we'd managed to duplicate them. No one had thought to ask whether we could stop posting out a hard copy now that the results were sent by email.

For me, it was a lesson in encouraging people to ask questions about every aspect of the businesses. As a leader, I need to create an environment where every staff member feels confident about asking questions. 'Why do we work that way?' 'Would it be more efficient if …?' 'Is it possible to …?' It's about creating openness and trust. And it's also about being prepared to listen.

At the education institution, the staff who distributed results were concerned that we were legislatively required to send out hard copies. We did our research and soon discovered that electronic distribution was sufficient. When we switched to electronic results only, we saved well over six-figures in printing and postage alone.

Keep your head on a swivel

When we went out on patrol in a combat zone, we always reminded our team to keep their heads on a swivel. We would collect information and assess the environment constantly. On patrol, there's no moment when you stop looking around and no moment when you stop paying attention. It's a constant process of question and response, of self-challenge combined with 'what if'. Dropping your guard for even a second could mean the difference between life or death. This is where the hyper-vigilant response is developed. There is so much information that you are trying to process, and at the same time you're trying to determine what is and what isn't life-threatening.

Business is the same, though thankfully less life-threatening. Leaders should always be listening, observing, assessing, and asking 'what if'. You need to scan the environment and be aware of what is happening – inside the organisation, amongst competitors, and in the wider industry. Be aware of local issues, but also watch for national and international developments. Listen to your workforce and what they are saying. Your job as a leader is to digest the information as quickly as possible and figure out how it matters to the business.

Avoid analysis paralysis

So, you're taking in all this information, analysing it, and thinking about how it applies to the business. How do you figure out what matters? How do you avoid becoming overwhelmed or paralysed by the options or the sheer volume of information?

Everyone has endless amounts of data available to them, and more information is only a key stroke away. You'll be bombarded by competitors' marketing and by information about your industry. You'll also be bombarded by internal issues and questions, including rumours and worries. Your job as a leader is to pull out only what matters for the decisions you need to take. You may need to make a split-second decision about whether something is important enough to attend to.

Try to challenge yourself about what information you're attending to. Step back and ask: Am I noticing the things that really matter? Am I paying attention where it's needed? Am I thinking through information that I can usefully apply? Am I listening to reliable sources that give me the whole story? Am I collecting enough detail to make good decisions?

My solution here is to take a mental step back. I try to remove myself from the situation just enough to make a reasoned, thoughtful, informed decision.

You cannot plan for every scenario

You can do all the planning in the world. You can imagine that you've thought through and addressed every possible scenario you will encounter. Then something will happen that you didn't expect. And that's why you can't plan yourself into complacency.

In the Army, we planned for pretty much every scenario we thought was likely to occur. But we also knew how we'd respond if we encountered something unexpected. We knew how to stop, access the damage, and make decisions about whether we were still mission capable. We always knew what it meant to be mission capable for anything we were trying to achieve.

Part of our planning in the Army meant that we always knew the capability of our resources and how to deploy them in any situation. We practised in drills so often that it became automatic. We all knew our own jobs. We knew the job of the next person in line, and we knew when and how to step in if needed. We knew when it was time to move out of a situation in order to preserve our resources to fight another day.

It's not so different in the workplace. In organisations, we need to monitor our progress, know what we're trying to achieve, and make active decisions about how to deploy our resources. Sometimes you might need to abandon a project because it's not working. What's important here is to make a balanced decision, based on the evidence. You can't get caught in the 'sunk cost fallacy' of worrying about the resources you've already invested into a project if it's increasingly clear that it's not going to work. Make sure you don't get so wrapped up in a project that you can't let go. Sometimes you must step back, cut your losses, and abandon the plan.

There's a myth that in the military we'll keep fighting until the last person is standing. This couldn't be further from the reality. This was probably true in earlier times but over time the value of the individual soldier has risen. We know that when we're getting hit bad, things are only going to get worse, particularly if we don't receive any immediate support. Recognising that our people are our greatest resource, no modern commanding officer is going to feed people into a battle that can't be won. People are a finite, limited, precious resource. We'll pull out and save our people for another day. However, we'll also come back with a new plan, and then we will win.

Understand people's capabilities and limitations

In Army combat situations, we put a lot of effort into planning the best way to deploy our resources. We made careful decisions about who would do what tasks, based on their strengths and capabilities. We planned in advance who would lead the team, who would kick down the door, who would provide cover, and so on. Our focus was how to use the team in the most efficient way to be successful and win the encounter. Then we'd train and train until we were ready to be deployed.

It's not that different in business. You need to understand people's strengths and limitations, then work to their strengths without pushing their weaknesses. Decide who to deploy for specific projects based on their strengths.

It usually doesn't make sense to allocate someone to a project because it will provide them with a learning opportunity or will address one of their weaknesses. That's likely to set them up for failure. It's also likely to bring that person an enormous amount of stress. Yes, you can do small things to help people address their weaknesses. But most of the time, it makes sense to capitalise on people's strengths.

If you use the most appropriate team with the best resources you can provide, you'll maximise their chances of success. Letting people play to their strengths is good for their morale and helps them to achieve autonomy over their work.

It's your job as a leader to set people up for success. Most people come to work wanting to be successful in their job. Whatever their job involves, most people want to feel that they're doing it successfully and that they're making a valuable contribution to the organisation.

People First

The NCO Creed has a lot to say about people:

My two basic responsibilities will always be uppermost in my mind – accomplishment of my mission and the welfare of my Soldiers ... All Soldiers are entitled to outstanding leadership; I will provide that leadership. I know my Soldiers, and I will always place their needs above my own. I will communicate consistently with my Soldiers and never leave them uninformed. I will be fair and impartial when recommending both rewards and punishment.

Officers of my unit will have maximum time to accomplish their duties; they will not have to accomplish mine. I will earn their respect and confidence as well as that of my Soldiers. I will be loyal to those with whom I serve; seniors, peers, and subordinates alike.

The second sentence above stands out most for me: *All Soldiers are entitled to outstanding leadership; I will provide that leadership.*

These days I take out the word 'soldiers' and replace it with 'employees' or 'people'. That sentence gives me the core of leadership. Three words are particularly important to me:

1. *Entitled* – the Creed doesn't say that people can 'ask for' leadership or they 'want' leadership. It says

they're 'entitled' to it. Simply by being a soldier or an employee – by giving their time to the organisation – people are entitled to leadership.
2. *Outstanding* – the Creed doesn't say that people are entitled to 'average' leadership, or 'no' leadership, or even to 'competent' leadership. They are entitled to 'outstanding' leadership: the best leadership that can be provided.
3. *I* – the Creed demands that the person who is reciting it – I – will provide the outstanding leadership required. If I put myself forward for a leadership position, then I must be willing to step up and accept the responsibility that comes with leadership. It's OK for me to seek training or professional development, but I must be willing to accept responsibility.

Just two responsibilities

The NCO Creed reminds me that leaders only have two responsibilities:
- I am responsible for achieving the organisation's strategy
- I am responsible for the welfare of my people.

These two responsibilities should guide every decision a leader makes. Any time I face a difficult decision, I stop and ask two questions: Does this support achieving the organisation's strategy? Is this best for the organisation's people?

These questions keep me focused. I don't ask what's best for shareholders, what's best for short-term cost-cutting, or what's best for the leadership team. I don't ask what will make my life easier or what will satisfy noisy stakeholders. These things might all be relevant, but they should never be as important as my two key responsibilities – the organisation's strategy and the organisation's people.

Good leadership is selfless. My needs and my interests are less relevant than the needs and interests of my team. Taking care of the team – putting people first – should be the anchor of everything a leader does.

What if the two responsibilities conflict?

It's rare for a leader's responsibility to the organisation's strategy to conflict with the leader's responsibility to the organisation's people. But it can happen, particularly in an environment where you need to make tough decisions about redundancies or closures, for example.

Sometimes an organisation will change strategic direction, and this will be difficult for the people. Sometimes an organisation will exist in a volatile environment, and you'll need to make major changes to stay afloat. In these situations, you need to make the best decision you can while balancing the interests of the organisation's strategy and people.

In difficult circumstances, keep in mind that your responsibility is to the collective. You are responsible for the organisation's entire strategy and for all its people. At times, you'll need to make decisions that are difficult for individuals or small groups in order to meet your responsibility to everyone.

When you're forced to make difficult decisions, particularly decisions around redundancies, remember that these decisions are difficult for everyone. It's hard on you to make the decision and communicate it sensitively to staff. It's very hard on anyone who is at the receiving end of your decisions. Moving people out of an organisation is also very hard on the people who stay behind. It is also hard on people's families and communities. Always remember that behind every employee, there is someone else – a spouse, children, parents, siblings, and so on. I always keep this front of mind as I make decisions that steer the organisation or affect its sustainability.

If you're sensitive about difficult decisions and take your responsibilities seriously, you're more likely to communicate clearly about why you're making decisions that people find difficult to accept. Your commitment is to make sound decisions that maintain the viability of the entire business.

Don't avoid conflict

As a leader, you are responsible for everything that happens inside the organisation. And that means that you're the person who needs to act when things get difficult.

If you discover conflict inside the organisation, it's your responsibility to make sure it's addressed. Don't ignore it, and don't leave it to fester. Conflict can be a bit like organisational cancer: if you ignore it, it won't go away. It will simply get worse and may eventually become deadly.

No one wants to deal with conflict. It's confronting and difficult. Most people ignore it and hope it goes away. But if you're a leader you can't avoid it. You're the person who is paid to take responsibility for it and you owe it to the organisation to address it as quickly as possible. Every day that you ignore it is a day you're sending out a message that it's acceptable.

Like most people, I'm not comfortable when dealing with conflict. But I do it because I know that I have to. I know it has to be done and it's a responsibility I accepted when I accepted the job.

My success depends on my team

I don't hide the fact that most of my business success depends on my team. If I was to put a figure on it, I'd guess that more than 80 percent of my success rests with my team.

My job is to choose the right people and create an environment where they can succeed. I help to develop the vision and direction, and I make sure they have the tools to be successful. But the real success rests with them. And because the organisation's success rests with them, I'm responsible to them. It's my job to provide them with an enabling environment so that they can do their work.

I believe that leaders need to give people parameters and resources, and then get out of their way. They'll be more successful if they don't have constant monitoring from me. The more successful I can make my team, the more successful the organisation will be and in turn the more successful I will be.

Working to overcome resistance

Sometimes you'll be faced with people who resist change and criticise the organisation's direction. Try to think creatively about the best way to encourage their buy-in.

People who resist change are often worried about what the change will mean for them or concerned about learning something new. People often worry about whether they'll still have a job or whether they'll be capable of doing what they're asked. Change creates fear, and many people prefer to keep doing work that is familiar and well-understood.

You can help to overcome fear of change by listening to people's fears and communicating clearly about what the change will involve. You can help to develop familiarity and understanding through training and testing. Try to balance the organisation's need for change against the people's need for familiarity. Can you find a way to make the change process easier for people?

Increase people's sense of autonomy

In many organisations, lower-level jobs come with less pay and less control. Often, they also come with more stress. It's a lack of personal autonomy – of control over day-to-day work decisions – that often creates stress for people.

If you can find ways to give people autonomy in their work, you will reduce stress and give them higher levels of job satisfaction. The more experienced someone is at their job, the more autonomy they should be able to have.

I believe that, in most jobs, people should be paid for the work they accomplish, not for the hours and minutes they spend at work. This doesn't apply in organisations that need constant staffing (like hospitals or call centres), but in many work environments it makes sense to focus mostly on outcomes. If someone achieves everything that's asked of them in fewer hours than expected, they should be able to decide what to do with the extra time.

If your organisation prioritises clock-on time ahead of outcomes, or if your organisation excessively monitors staff behaviour, it's possible that staff will feel more stressed than necessary. It's also possible they'll respond by working more slowly than they otherwise would.

Here's an example. Suppose you manage a team of maintenance workers and grounds staff, and you've got some people who work off-site. Maybe they're employed to cut grass at parks or on grass verges. The off-site employees can be given autonomy in their work by being trusted with their start times, finish times, and breaks. It makes sense to monitor them for quality of work and amount of grass-cutting completed but monitoring for minutes worked will only remove any sense of control they feel. Additionally, monitoring for time is not a performance indicator that will lead to improved performance. What you should monitor in this example is the quality of the cutting. However, if you do find that your team isn't able to accomplish their tasks in a reasonable amount of time you need to investigate why.

Another example is the pilot of an airplane. I have some experience with this as I have a pilot's licence and enjoy flying as a hobby. Being a pilot is highly restrictive, with many regulations and processes that must be followed. When I'm in the cockpit, I need to follow the same regulations as all other pilots. The regulations guide how I can fly, where I can fly, and whom I can talk to. But whenever I'm in a plane, I'm 100 percent responsible for what happens. It's my job to get the plane to its destination safely. The rules of flying confine me and tell me what I can and can't do – just like a position description confines an employee. As a pilot, I'm out there doing the job I'm expected to do, and people expect me to perform it successfully.

In the plane and with the grass-cutting employee, there's no benefit in having someone monitoring that the job is being done right. In fact, most of the time ongoing monitoring is counter-productive. The pilot (or employee) can be so distracted by being watched all the time that they begin to make mistakes.

As a leader, I don't pay people to be seat-warmers – that is, to just show up for work. People's pay is linked to the value they bring, and people are paid to complete a task. Just by completing the task properly, they've accomplished the requirements of their job. Of course, I want people to be efficient, but in most cases I don't need them to work set hours.

Empower people then get out of their way

Leadership is about empowering people – with vision, motivation, training, and resources – and then getting out of the way and letting them get on with the job. You might give people guidelines, and you might give people parameters to work within, but then you let them drive their own work forward.

If you give people some autonomy over their work, and if you avoid the temptation to constantly monitor every aspect of what they do, you'll help to develop competent, independent workers who can manage in your absence. You'll be able to take leave, knowing that the organisation can manage. You'll also develop your team's managerial and leadership potential, so they can move up through the organisation and build their careers.

One part of empowering staff is making sure they understand the limits of the risks they can take. People in managerial roles need to understand what their risk budget is – this is their freedom to make independent decisions that place some risk on money or resources. Decision-making is nearly always a gamble – hopefully a calculated gamble made after gathering information, but still a gamble. It's important that leaders let their staff take calculated risks, and that you then support them if things go wrong.

In one organisation I worked with, we transitioned to a new data-management system. The organisation operates in a remote region with limited availability of resources. However, all of the procurement is now based in the cloud. This is a business risk, particularly in a remote location with internet access that can be unreliable. It may fail. It may not meet the needs of the organisation. It might not operate the right way for us. But it was a calculated risk to move to the cloud, based on the information we had at the time. And in the scheme of things, in the overall context of what the organisation does, it's a very small risk. It's helpful to calculate the real risk of decisions. Most decisions might cause damage or upset, but that can be managed. True risk will destroy the organisation or damage the workforce. They're the risks you need to avoid.

We're all on the same team

We used to say that we're all green in the Army. It was our way of saying that, when you're wearing an Army uniform, you're all part of the same team. We're alike and united by our uniform, our discipline, and our commitment.

But being on the same team doesn't mean that we're not different. We might look the same – with our uniforms, short haircuts, and high levels of fitness. But we don't think the same. We don't process information the same way. In the Army, we're alike but we're also diverse. We have different backgrounds, different values, different religions, different cultures. And it's that diversity of perspective that brings strength to our work.

In the workplace, remember that diversity brings in creative thinking and new ideas. It also helps to prevent bad decisions which can be caused by everyone thinking the same way and failing to challenge the norm.

You're not going to like everyone you work with, and the people you work with won't all like you. But you're work colleagues, not friends. Even though you think differently to someone else, you can still be professional about it. You can still treat people with dignity and respect. And you can still work on the same team.

Every soldier is a sensor

In the Army we had a program where we focused on ways to gather information from all our people. The idea was that every soldier in the field was sensing their environment and gathering useful data. Because we all noticed different things, we could combine our insights and use the information to our benefit. Instead of asking unit leaders to make decisions based on their own narrow perspectives, we had everyone's perspectives feeding into the mix. Then we could look for themes and common threads, develop useful intelligence, and take action.

One time in Iraq, I was on a patrol and we were hit by an improvised explosive device – an IED. Thankfully it wasn't very powerful and went off between two vehicles. We had some minor vehicle damage, but no injuries. Well, nothing more serious than ringing ears. We immediately took evasive action, eliminated the threat of any further actions by the insurgents, and continued with our patrol. When we got back to base, we completed an after-action review – an AAR – just like we did every time something happened.

In an AAR, everyone who is in some way involved in the action gets involved in the review. We review every aspect, from the control briefing and the starting point, right through to the end. Operating under the idea that every soldier is a sensor, we ask everyone to talk through the details of what they say and what they think happened.

After a series of AARs following hits like the one we'd experienced, we started to notice a pattern. We were being set up, and trigger operators were being alerted to our arrival. It was a simple strategy, but it took us a while to notice the pattern. They would pull a vehicle to the side of the road, pretending it was broken down. As we approached, the driver would get out of the vehicle and lift the hood. That would alert the trigger operators to our arrival. It was then very simple for the trigger operators to detonate the device when we got close.

In another area, we used the same process to discover a different warning technique. A particular pattern of rocks on the side of the road were being used to mark an IED, usually about 100 metres out. Once we learned the pattern, we could predict with a high degree of accuracy what was ahead. That gave us the insights needed to change our tactics and try something different.

Most businesses are no different from these military examples. You and your team need to constantly watch for themes and patterns and decide when it's time to do things differently. If you see your employees and your customers as sensors and you create opportunities to gather information, you'll be able to vastly increase your opportunities to respond to what you learn.

I currently live in a remote community, and part of my work involves helping the local hospital board to look for patterns and themes that suggest we need to act. The hospital staff noticed that they see more head injuries than the state average, largely because people don't wear helmets when they're riding on their massive properties. Once our sensors had noticed the theme, we could begin to work on ways to address the problem, through a combination of consumer education and industry advocacy.

Create a disciplined culture, but don't dispense discipline

A disciplined culture is not the same as a culture where discipline is readily dispensed.

In the Army, we were highly disciplined. We knew what was expected of us, and when. We could work in the absence of supervision. If someone was taken out through injury, the next person in line knew how to step up and take command.

The best leaders in the Army didn't dispense discipline through punishment and blame or through excessive reward. The best leaders would support us if something went wrong and would help us find ways to bring things to rights. Then, when things had settled down enough, they would sit down and talk with us about what had happened and what could be done differently. Those leaders helped us to learn and develop our careers. They didn't establish a culture of fear or blame.

The last thing a leader should do is lay blame on other people. It creates a culture of fear, where people follow orders because they worry about the consequences. That's not a path to creativity or good decision-making.

As I was transitioning out of the Army, I kept encountering the stereotype that I must be a strong disciplinarian. People expected me to yell at staff, demand attention, and require absolute obedience. I think people have seen too much coverage of the war on terrorism, and they expect all military personnel to be kicking in doors, shooting randomly, messed up with PTSD, and just one step away from snapping in the workplace.

That's not me at all, and it's probably not like most veterans. I don't yell at people, and I was rarely yelled at in the Army. I don't expect blind obedience. As a matter of fact, I discourage blind obedience. I expect clear-thinking, committed staff who have the organisation's best interests at heart. I expect to be treated with dignity and respect. And in return I promise to treat everyone I meet with dignity and respect.

In the Army, we were highly self-disciplined because that's what we were trained to be. The best of our self-disciplined leaders didn't ever resort to dispensing discipline through punishment or blame. They didn't need to.

Invest in your team

If you want your team to be effective and efficient, it makes sense to invest money in the best resources you can offer. Find out whether your people have access to the systems and equipment they need to be successful. Do some research about what is needed – both by the organisation and by the individual.

Investing in your team is not simply about sending them to a conference or training program. That's just one part of it. True investment is providing the resources and the environment they need to perform successfully in their work.

I once had a team working in a poorly maintained, antiquated office. I was concerned that the ceiling would fall in or that they'd suffer sickness from exposure to mould. This team found it very difficult to be efficient because their work environment influenced what they could do. I was able to move the team into a renovated office with plenty of light and new furniture. What that move did for staff morale and productivity was incredible. The improved productivity more than paid for the cost of the move. In that situation, the team was not in control of their work environment and its effect on them was obvious. By leaving them there, the organisation gave the impression that they didn't care.

What about team-building activities?

I'm in two minds about team-building activities in the workplace. They're often done with the best of intentions. But you have to question whether they matter to the people involved, and you need to think about what you're trying to achieve.

Organisations come up with all sorts of programs – like morning teas, wellness challenges, social events, and team-building sessions. People might be enthusiastic for a while, but then you'll start to hear grumbling because people don't want to be involved. Once the grumbling starts, it's possible that the program is actually counterproductive. It might be worse than doing nothing at all.

Social events can be particularly difficult. They often fail because they're a form of mandatory fun. People feel they have to be involved, whether they want to or not. You're trying to bring together all sorts of different personalities, suddenly asking people to socialise together when they're used to working together.

Another problem with team-building activities can be related to span and control. If you try team-building at a high level – with too many people involved or across large chunks of the organisation – it's not going to work. Team-building might make sense at the local level, with between seven and twelve people deciding on something that makes sense for them. But it often becomes ineffective if it's expanded throughout the organisation.

Workplace morning teas are a good example here. They work well in small groups where people get together to celebrate something in their team. If another team sees what's happening and decides to have their own morning tea, then that's a good thing. But if an executive sees multiple morning teas happening and decides to combine them all into one large morning tea each month – where everyone's birthdays are celebrated and everyone's achievements are named – it quickly becomes a disaster. The large morning tea loses the intimacy and meaning of the team-based activity and quickly becomes a work function to be endured. It doesn't matter whether there's a little morning tea happening every day somewhere in the organisation. What matters is that it's done at the small team level, in a way that supports team interaction. These things are better kept small and organic.

Sometimes you might want to show up to a group's morning tea or team-building activity. It's great when a senior leader shows they're interested in the team. But if you do that, make sure you have a reason for being there – a reason that's linked to the team's work and the team's achievements, not linked to something you want to say.

Show gratitude

I once had a supervisor who didn't believe in showing gratitude. One time when I was working for him, I received a report from a team member. I remember the person handing the report to me, me saying thanks, and the person then walking away. My supervisor pulled me into his office and berated me for it. He said you should never thank someone for doing their job. That's what they're being paid to do, and you should just expect it to be done.

I was dumbfounded by his attitude. It's one of the most ridiculous things I've ever heard to suggest that you shouldn't thank someone for good work. A person might be paid to do a job, but that's no reason to avoid saying thanks for work well done. That person could easily do the job badly or late. And they could easily go and work somewhere else. To me, it makes good sense to say thanks.

In most cases, the best gratitude is simple, authentic, and unplanned. Notice good work. Say thank you. Do what you can to show people you value and appreciate their efforts. Real gratitude is motivating – it creates teams who want to work with you and it helps encourage people to go the extra mile for you. It's the polar opposite of trying to motivate people using threats.

Hire people who are smarter than you

When you're building a team in the workplace, hire to fill skills gaps. As much as possible, try to hire people who are smarter than you or who will bring the skills that you lack.

As a leader, you should be honest with yourself about what your skills void is. We all have one. Mine is that I'm not a particularly strong finance person. Then, when you're hiring people to be your direct reports, hire people who will help to plug the gap in your skills. I work with a very strong finance person who reports directly to me. That person helps to make sure I'm on top of the detail. Together, we make a great team.

Often when I'm new to an organisation, I'll be told that someone isn't very good at their job and I'll probably need to let them go. When I'm new, I always say that I will do my own assessment before making any decisions. That's the time I need to get to know the organisation before making any change. So often, I notice that the person being complained about has valuable skills but has been employed into the wrong job. If someone has skills that can't be used in their job, they're not likely to be a good fit. My first choice is always to move that person to a different position where they're able to use their skills and contribute to the organisation. Most of the time, it's like setting them on a launch pad. They're off! It happens because I've moved them to a role where they can use their strengths and because I've shown that I believe in investing in them. It's like they were full of rocket fuel, and suddenly I've lit them up.

Hire for attitude, ahead of skill

When you're hiring new people into the organisation, attitude is the most important attribute to look for. Skills and qualifications are important, but they're never enough. You want to find a person with the attitude, drive, motivation, and strategic thinking to fit with your team. You can usually help people to develop the right skills through training and mentoring. Attitude is more difficult to change.

In job interviews, I try to ask questions that will uncover the applicant's attitude. I'm usually part of an interviewing panel, and one of my strategies is to always sit at the side. If I'm on the side of the group, I can see both the interviewee and the other panel members. I like to watch their nonverbal responses to get an idea of how comfortable they are. I also like to ask situational questions that help me understand something about the type of person we're interviewing. For example, I might ask what their previous supervisor would say if I asked for their worst quality and their best quality. I also like to ask an open question, like: 'What's your experience with x…?', and then keep quiet and wait for the person to talk. Most people will speak to fill the void, and their answers can be really useful for uncovering attitude.

I once heard of an interviewer who asked each interviewee what they'd do if they opened the office refrigerator and found a penguin inside. The interview was for an executive assistant role, and they were looking for someone who would research where the penguin had come from, why it was there, and where it should be. Anyone who answered that they would take a photograph of the penguin and post it to Instagram was better suited to marketing than to an executive assistant role. I'm in two minds about questions like these. You want to uncover attitude, but you don't want to throw people off or ask something that's too left of field.

In most interviews, you have people from the organisation sitting on one side of the table and the lone applicant sitting on the other side. The organisation spends much of the time in the interview asking a series of questions in order to assess whether the candidate is suitable for the organisation. Toward the end of the interview, the candidate can ask a few questions. Typically, the questions that both the interviewer and the interviewee ask are stock standard. The problem with this format is that anyone can practise answering questions and you don't get a good feel for the candidate's true personality.

If you really want to assess someone's attitude or personality, then you need to get them into a more social situation.

In some situations, it might make sense to introduce job applicants to other members of the team – perhaps by joining the team for morning tea or for lunch. Watching people in a social situation can be helpful for assessing attitude. It's probably only fair to do this if the applicant knows in advance that they'll be invited to lunch (or whatever social event you choose). Once a candidate gets into a more social situation, they will relax a bit more. Watch how they interact with others. You will then be able to determine whether they are a good fit for your organisation.

Hire for where you're going, not for where you are

Organisations need to hire staff who will help achieve their strategic goals and meet the needs of where the company expects to be in the future. It's important to match the organisation's skills matrix with the goals outlined in the strategic plan.

In many organisations, there's a rush to fill a position any time someone leaves. At some point in the organisation's history, a leader decided to employ someone to do a particular task. Any time someone leaves that role, a new hire is made into that position without evaluating whether the role is still relevant.

Any time a person resigns, they're providing the organisation with an opportunity to review the role. Do you still need that position? Is the level right? Are the skill requirements still current? Is that position helping to fulfill the organisation's strategic goals?

Ideally, you'll be regularly reviewing positions and strategic job families across the organisation. Ask whether you've got the right positions to fill current market conditions. Ask whether your workforce is able to adapt to the conditions you see lying ahead. If not, what can you do to fix it? Do we need to bring in new skills? In most cases, this won't be a conversation about planned redundancies. It's more likely to be a conversation about skills development and futureproofing. If you have the right resources, you're more likely to achieve the organisation's objectives.

Leadership isn't for everyone

Not everyone in your organisation will aspire to hold a leadership position. And not everyone who aspires to leadership will have the skills or capacity needed for it.

Technical skills and leadership skills are not the same, and it's quite possible that someone who is at the top of their game from a technical perspective will not make a great leader. Don't make the mistake of promoting a technically excellent person into a leadership position if that's not what they want and not where they'll perform well.

You may be familiar with the Peter Principle – the management concept developed by Laurence J Peter which suggests that most people get promoted to the level of their incompetence. The Peter Principle suggests that many organisations have leaders who are working beyond the level where they should be. A related idea popularised by Tom Schuller is the Paula Principle – the idea that women tend to work below their level of competence.

In choosing people for leadership positions, it's important to stay alert to the risks of both the Peter Principle and the Paula Principle. Look for potential leaders who are motivated and skilled in leadership. Don't assume that technical experts will automatically make great leaders, and don't assume that people who are quiet about their achievements shouldn't become leaders.

There are some people who do not want the responsibility that comes with a leadership role. It can be stressful, and it isn't for everyone. I have found that many people crave leadership, but do not wish to be the leader themselves. They look to leaders to provide them with direction and to make decisions.

I used to work in a health research organisation, where we employed some incredible researchers with very strong international reputations. Many of those researchers wanted to conduct research, without taking on leadership responsibilities. One of the challenges in research is that researchers can extend their impact by expanding their team and supervising junior researchers. With that comes leadership responsibility. It's almost as though leadership responsibility is the consequence of success. In the organisation, we handled this problem by providing resources to support senior researchers, enabling them to be research leaders without taking on the administrative responsibilities of a leadership position.

Keep in touch with your people

It's important to remember that our teams are made up of whole, complex people with partners, children, and lives outside work. You don't need to know everything about your staff, and you certainly don't need to be their best friend, but it's useful to know them as people and to have some understanding of what makes them tick.

If you keep in touch with your staff, you'll be more likely to notice if things suddenly change. If things are bad at work, your staff are going to take it home. Equally, if things are bad at home, it will be carried into their work. If you have a good relationship with your staff, you'll be better able to ask if something is wrong.

Having difficulties at home isn't an excuse for performing poorly at work, but it does provide an explanation and will help you to understand. Then you can decide what to do, based on your understanding. Maybe you'll be able to offer some useful support.

Keeping in touch with your people – in a way that's open, supportive, transparent, and fair – can go a long way in supporting people's work–life balance and in helping with staff retention.

Assume that people are well-intentioned

It's helpful to assume that the majority of people have good intentions and most people want to do a good job. Most of the people I meet go to work every day expecting to do the best they can. They want to accomplish the tasks they were employed to do, to the best of their ability. Most people are not lazy and most people do not cut corners. If you assume that people have good intentions, you'll be more likely to give them the respect and space they need to do their job well.

By assuming the best in people, you might sometimes get caught out. You're putting faith in people that they're there to do the right thing. And maybe not everyone will. But most will, and you don't want to punish the majority to control the few. Instead, hunt out those few and remove them from your organisation.

How hard can you push?

One of the difficulties facing a leader is to know how much to push or challenge the team. Your goal is to push hard enough to create a motivating challenge but not so hard that the challenge seems impossible. Too much stress and people will crack. Too little stress and people become bored.

In the weight room, I increase stress by tiny increments. It's highly quantitative and I can measure exactly what I'm doing.

Unfortunately, the work environment isn't quantitative like the weight room. It's qualitative, and leaders learn from experience how much stress to provide. An experienced leader will monitor people's stress levels and adjust the stress as needed. Sometimes you'll need to reduce stress by offering support or bringing in more resources. Sometimes you'll need to reduce stress by forcing people to say no. And at other times you'll see an opportunity to ramp up the stress just a little to create an opportunity for someone who is ready for a challenge.

Build Trust and Confidence

The NCO Creed says:

Officers in my unit will have maximum time to accomplish their duties; they will not have to accomplish mine. I will earn their respect and confidence as well as that of my Soldiers. I will be loyal to those with whom I serve; seniors, peers, and subordinates alike.

Don't demand respect; earn it

When you're in a leadership position, you have a certain level of authority simply by virtue of the position you're in. But authority doesn't necessarily equate to respect. True respect is something you earn, by consistently building trust and confidence amongst your team. As the NCO Creed so clearly points out, trust and confidence are earned, not given as a right and not demanded.

Respect is ultimately a by-product of trust, confidence, good decisions and sound judgement. To earn respect, leaders need to work consciously and consistently to deserve and generate both trust and confidence.

Chief Executive Officer? Try Chief Cultural Officer

Sometimes it's helpful to think of the CEO, or any senior executive, as being the organisation's CCO – the Chief Cultural Officer. Organisational culture is one of those slippery things that seems difficult to define and difficult to address. You know when an organisation's culture is positive and strong because people are happy about coming to work and confident about what the organisation is trying to achieve. But putting your finger on just what causes or influences the culture might not be so easy.

Ultimately, it's the CEO who is 100 percent responsible for organisational culture. Culture starts at the top of the organisation, and it's the CEO's responsibility to get it right. Even if cultural issues seem to sit within particular teams or seem confined to specific pockets of the organisation, it's the CEO who must take responsibility. Remember, you can, and should, delegate your authority but you can never delegate your responsibility. If you're a CEO or senior executive, the buck stops with you!

The board's responsibility for organisational culture

The board isn't involved in everyday operations, so its direct influence on organisational culture is likely to be minimal. But the board employs the CEO, and the CEO is 100 percent responsible for organisational culture.

Boards can support a strong organisational culture by:
- Monitoring culture, ideally using reliable tools that provide a combination of quantitative and qualitative data. Quantitative measures are unlikely to be enough; the board needs to look at the narratives that sit behind the numbers.

- Helping to explore the underlying issues. It makes sense for the board to look for trends and themes and to be part of the conversation about what things might be influencing organisational culture.
- Supporting the CEO. The CEO might need support to develop and implement ideas that will strengthen the organisational culture. It's the board's role to support the CEO in whatever way is needed.
- Bringing in outside help if it's needed. If the CEO is struggling to understand or address organisational culture issues, the board may decide to bring in help from an independent consultant or other expert.
- Taking action at the highest level if needed. If the CEO is unable or unwilling to take action, or if the CEO is the source of the problem, the board needs to take appropriate action.

What if you don't fit in?

Not everyone your organisation hires will be a good fit. The flip side to this is that it's impossible for you to be the right fit for every organisation you might work for. If you're employed directly into a leadership position from outside the organisation, it can be difficult to know in advance whether you're the right person for the job, no matter how thorough the interview process was or how much research you've done. That's what your probationary period is for. During probation, you need to evaluate the organisation, just as they need to evaluate you. You'll need to not only decide whether the organisation is a good fit for you but also you'll need to determine what your chances for success are in your new role.

If you notice that you're not fitting into the organisation, take some time to assess what's going on. It's possible that you don't have the skills they need. It's possible that the role isn't quite what you expected. It's also possible that there's a disconnect between you and other senior executives within the organisation.

At times, you'll find an organisational culture that needs to change and you'll be just the right person to turn it around. If you can bring in the right people and work to address cultural issues, then you're probably the right person to create change for that organisation.

But at other times, the cultural problems might be things that you can't address. Make a realistic assessment of whether you're the right person for the role and whether it's going to be possible for you to achieve success. If it's not going to work, don't stay past the time of your probation or any longer than you must. This may seem extreme but there's no point in staying somewhere if you're not the right person for the job. It will be a tough decision but in the long run you'll be in a much better place.

This happened to me once, when I accepted a senior leadership position. The organisational culture was not a good fit with my way of working, there were a number of decisions being made by the board that didn't sit comfortably for me. These decisions were not only unethical, they could also cause some serious legal issues. I went back to the NCO Creed, which says: *I will not compromise my integrity nor my moral courage.* Their ways of working did not align with my values, and I decided I wasn't the right person for the job.

Use authority appropriately

People in leadership positions hold a certain level of authority. When you are in a position of authority, there is no difference between asking or telling someone to do something. Regardless of how you put the task to them, they will feel obligated to do it. However, it is how you put the task to them and whether they feel they have the power to respond that makes a difference.

If a leader asks a team member to jump, in most cases the person will either ask 'how high?' or will simply start jumping. Rarely will the person ask 'why'. But that doesn't mean it's OK to ask without explaining why. People need to understand why they are doing what they're being asked to do. A little understanding goes a long way.

Good leaders should create an environment where two things happen as a matter of course. Firstly, if the leader says, 'please jump', the employee should jump with confidence because they trust the leader to make sensible, meaningful, useful requests. Secondly, if the leader says, 'please jump' and the employee isn't sure what to do or why, the employee should feel confident enough to ask questions because they work in an environment where questions are welcomed.

Good leaders use their authority appropriately and create an organisational culture that's based on trust and respect.

What not to do

I once heard of a CEO who made a habit of phoning staff at all hours of the day or night asking them to do supposedly urgent tasks. One time, the CEO asked a staff member to come into the office and attend to some emergency paperwork, even though the staff member was on annual leave.

The phone call went something like this: 'I understand that you're on leave and you can say no to this if you want to. But I have this urgent matter that needs to be addressed and you're the only person who can do it properly. Will you come in today and do it?'

The CEO has supposedly given the employee permission to say no to this request. But most employees will feel that the CEO's authority makes this an instruction, not a request.

Most people will not say no, even though they're being asked to do something unreasonable. It's important that leaders don't make a habit of exercising authority inappropriately.

In the end, the task wasn't urgent and could have waited until the employee returned from leave. This left the employee feeling disgruntled as it took time away from their leave and their family.

Remember, entitlements such as leave are not just a privilege but an earned right. They have accrued leave in return for the hard work they have already put in. Allow them to take their leave and protect their time away. People need time away from work to allow themselves to recharge. If you give the courtesy of not being bothered, they will come back reenergised, happier and more productive.

Create an environment where people can ask questions and say no

Most employees do not feel they have the power to say no or ask questions when the CEO asks them to do something. It's your job, as the leader, to create an environment where this is not only OK, it's expected.

It will take some time to create this environment if staff are not used to it. You may need to challenge staff or encourage them to say no. Sometimes you may need to say no on their behalf.

The worst thing is to offer someone an option and then overrule their choice. This will simply undermine any sense they have that they're able to make choices. If they say 'no', say 'ok thanks, it can wait'.

Dig deep – find out what's behind the problem

If something isn't being done efficiently or well, it's important to dig into the issue and find out what's really going on.

Sometimes the problem you're seeing is simply the symptom of a deeper problem.

I was once part of a well-functioning board, but suddenly the CEO seemed to lose focus. As a board, we weren't involved in the company's day-to-day operations, so the only symptom we saw was that the board papers were suddenly running late, the CEO was disorganised and we weren't getting the information we needed to make informed decisions. Instead of getting the board papers well in advance so that we could prepare for the meeting, we started to get the board papers just a few hours ahead. We suddenly didn't have the time we needed to fully read and digest the board papers.

In this situation, we could have complained and demanded that the CEO improve his attention to detail. But instead we asked an open question about whether something had changed or whether there was a problem we didn't know about. It turned out that the CEO was distracted and stressed: he had a close family member who had been diagnosed with terminal cancer, and the CEO was flying to see them every weekend.

As a board, we then understood the reason behind the problem. The reason isn't an excuse, but understanding the reason gave us an opportunity to think about how to fix it. In this situation, we knew it was going to be a protracted timeframe, we asked the board's secretary to step up and help out a bit more with the CEO's work in preparing for the board meetings. Additionally, we were able to step up one of the senior executives into a deputy CEO role to share some of the load until the situation was remedied.

The lesson for our board was that we found a successful solution because we didn't jump to conclusions. We didn't blame the CEO and demand improved timeliness. Instead, we asked questions before making a decision and found a solution that provided temporary support to the CEO and improved the board's relationship with him. It taught me how important it is for board members to look for clues about what's going on inside the organisation, and then to dig deep if something doesn't look right.

It's not OK to be late

We had a saying in the Army that the person who is in charge is never late. The idea was that the person chairing the meeting was the most time poor. Whenever that person showed up to start the meeting, that was the start time. Everyone else should be waiting.

This is not a practical, fair way of working. Everyone is time poor, everyone is busy, and everyone is trying to get a job done. So simple respect suggests that meetings should start on time and end on time. It's everyone's responsibility to be organised enough to arrive for meetings on time. Show your employees some courtesy and be on time for them!

Respect working hours

As a leader, you may choose to work long hours. That's your choice. Just don't expect other staff members to make the same choice. And make sure you don't indicate to staff that you expect them to work crazy hours.

Technology creates a problem here. Because we have access to technology at all hours, it's easy to contact staff when we shouldn't. A respectful leader demonstrates that they respect people's time by not sending email at night, not sending email on weekends, not calling them after hours, and not contacting them when they're on leave.

If you make a habit of respecting working hours, you'll probably find that staff are much more willing to help when a genuine emergency happens. I call these the 'life, limb, or eyesight' occasions. They're the times when people are genuinely in danger. When that happens, of course it's OK to make contact out of hours. But if it's not absolutely critical, it will wait. The thing to remember here is that you have to let your staff know what type of emergencies you need to be contacted out of hours for, so there's no hesitation on their part.

Learning my own lesson

One time when I started in a new role, I realised that I was breaking my own rule about respecting people's time. I decided to put aside a bit of time every Sunday afternoon to plan for the week ahead. I'd find somewhere quiet at home, gather my thoughts, and plan what needed to be done that week. Then I'd email the relevant staff, setting out my thoughts and lining up meetings.

I expected that staff would respond to my messages when they arrived at work on Monday morning. But almost straight away, I started to get emails back from people. They were responding to my requests and getting on with the job, even though it was Sunday afternoon. I replied immediately, letting them know that I didn't expect a response until Monday.

The next week came around and the same thing happened. I gathered my thoughts on Sunday afternoon, sent out a few emails, and almost immediately started to get replies. The staff didn't believe me when I said that things could wait until Monday, and my Sunday afternoon emails reinforced that perception.

To fix this issue, I changed the way I work. I still gather my thoughts on a Sunday afternoon, and I still write emails to staff. But instead of sending them, I now save them as drafts. I don't press send until 8:00 am on Monday morning. My new approach helps to stop my team feeling anxious that I expect them to work on Sunday afternoons. It also means that I'm reinforcing my expectations through the way I behave.

How to decide if an issue is truly critical

When you're in the midst of dealing with an issue, it is likely to seem critically important. You're focused and engaged. Solving whatever is happening seems like the most important thing to be done.

Before deciding that your issue is critical and you need staff to drop everything else to help you solve it, stop and challenge yourself. Is this issue *truly* critical? Three questions are relevant:

1. Will someone be injured or killed if we don't address this now?
2. Will someone be significantly disadvantaged if we don't address this now?
3. Will the business stop functioning if we don't address this now?

If the answer to these questions is 'no', then your issue is probably not truly critical and you can probably take a measured approach in dealing with it.

Don't start conversations with 'sorry to bother you but'

When you start a conversation with 'sorry to bother you but', you're pretending to apologise for the interruption. But you're most likely communicating that you're not sorry at all because your issue or topic is more important than whatever the other person was doing.

If you're genuinely concerned about whether this is an appropriate time to talk, consider saying 'is this a good time for me to ask about …' or 'can you spare me a few minutes to discuss …'. Then listen to the answer you get back, and only launch into the conversation if the other person gives you permission. If the other person says it's not a convenient time to talk, you need to respect that.

I was at a restaurant once with a CEO who noticed one of his employees sitting nearby with his family. The CEO called this employee over to us and said, 'I'm sorry to bother you, and I know you're on leave, but I just need to ask you about a work issue for a minute'. But it's never a minute, is it? The conversation went on for about 30 minutes, with the employee's family waiting for him at the table, their family dinner interrupted. The CEO wasn't asking about anything important. He just saw an opportunity to talk about something that was on his mind, and he didn't stop to think about the message he was sending to the employee and the employee's family.

Sometimes you need to force people to take time off

Sometimes people get so caught up in what they're doing that they don't take time off and they don't look after themselves. If they're enjoying the task or the situation is temporary, then it's unlikely to be a problem. But as a leader you need to be alert for signs that a staff member is out of their depth or struggling to cope.

I once had a senior manager reporting to me who had been struggling for some time and clearly needed some support. This person was struggling with anxiety at work and experiencing complex situations in his personal life that were weighing heavily on him. I could see that the long hours and stress were taking their toll. He was constantly playing catch up as he fell behind in both areas, becoming unfocused and ineffective in his job.

I tried a few different support strategies and nothing seemed to work. So eventually I laid down some rules. I told this manager that if I saw evidence of him checking his email or making work calls either after 6:00 pm, before 7:00 am, or at any time on the weekend, it could lead to his dismissal. It sounded as though I was threatening to fire him for doing his job!

In reality I was helping him to find some balance and giving him time back to address his personal issues. He was only an asset to the organisation if he was focused and well rested. He was a good manager and I didn't want to lose him. I particularly didn't want him to burn out.

Our initial conversation didn't go too well. The manager thought he was being punished and he didn't appreciate what I was asking him to do. But after a few weeks, I could see him returning to his former self. After about a month, he thanked me for forcing him to make the change.

If an employee suffers from excess stress or has a breakdown, it's ultimately the leader's responsibility. As a leader, you need to assess whether staff have an appropriate workload. You need to check whether they've got the right resources and the most appropriate training. It's your job to set them up for success so they have some longevity with your organisation.

You're standing in someone's way

If you're employed in a leadership position inside an organisation, you're in a job that someone else could do. You're probably supervising people who aspire to advance their careers and take your job. There's nothing unusual about this; in just about every job you take, you'll be standing in someone else's career path and preventing someone else from getting promoted.

If you employ a strong team of high performers, you're likely to employ people who seek promotion. And if your organisation doesn't have opportunities available at the right time, that person is likely to look outside. This is a good sign, and you should embrace it positively, even though it may be disruptive. It's helpful to see your team's advancement as a sign of your success as a leader and mentor because you've helped this person to develop their skills to the point of being ready for promotion.

If possible, support people who move on to positions in other organisations by being a partner in the process. Work with them and help to develop their networks. Be professional and keep in touch. You never know when your paths will cross again.

I've worked with many people who outgrew our organisation, and I've helped them to develop their networks and find new opportunities. It's incredible to keep in touch with these people and see how far their careers can go. It's not about them being in competition with me. It's about watching them advance and make great contributions to other organisations, knowing that I've been part of their journey.

The LinkedIn headhunters

I remember having a conversation one day with our CFO. She was upset because several of her staff were being chased by headhunters through LinkedIn. Most of them were being looked at for roles that were a higher level than the ones they were currently in. I could see why she was upset and anxious about the possibility of losing great staff. I gave her three pieces of advice about the situation:

1. View the situation as a great source of pride. Like the old saying goes, 'all the good people work for someone else'. Well, if recruiting agencies are trying to steal

away most of your staff, then all the good people must work for you!
2. If your staff are happy and you're providing them with great leadership, they are more likely to stay and not leave.
3. Some people will be ready to move and take roles with more responsibility. This is a reflection of the time and effort she had spent in developing them to be the best they could be. She should not hold this against them, but rather work with them and support them along their career path.

Develop your staff

We all want to feel needed. But a good leader will develop their staff and give them some freedom so that the organisation can operate well in their absence. Everyone is replaceable, including you.

In the Army, we operated on the understanding that we could always work two levels above our current position or one level below. If my immediate supervisor was unavailable or injured, I could step into their position. And if I became unavailable or injured myself, the person who reported to me would step in. To achieve this, the Army was always developing people to move up.

I once reported to a senior executive who did a great job of developing her team. She empowered us all and communicated well, so we understood exactly what decisions we could make in her absence. We also understood that if we made a decision that didn't work out well it would be used as a learning opportunity not as an opportunity for punishment. The leadership team was cohesive. We were all experts in our fields, empowered to speak up and empowered to make decisions. This was probably one of the best teams I ever had the pleasure of working with.

Be consistent

Organisations need leaders to be consistent and stable. If you're consistent in your leadership style and decision-making approach, you'll create confidence and stability within your team. Consistency helps to reduce confusion and anxiety. Your team can become familiar with how you make decisions and begin to anticipate the questions you'll ask.

I've worked in some organisations where people need to start each day by asking the CEO's executive assistant which CEO has arrived at work that day. You know the type – one day they're fair and reasonable, but the next day they hate the world and make erratic decisions. Do everything possible to be consistent and stable. Remember that people learn from you and try to anticipate how you'll react. If you lead based on your mood, then it will be hard for you to be consistent. Your staff need you to be steady, sure, and consistent. Consistency will help to bring a calmness to your team, even when you face stressful situations.

I once had a supervisor who was consistent around 90 percent of the time. But every so often he'd come into the office and act like a real jerk – yelling at everyone as loudly as he could and even knocking things off people's desks in anger. I asked him about why he acted this way and he said he did it on purpose to keep people on their toes. People were kept on their toes all right, but from fear that they might be the next target of his anger.

Don't forget that being consistent in your actions does not mean you are emotionless. It means that your emotions are under control. It is okay to be human and show emotions. The more human you are, the more trust people will have in you. Just don't let your emotions get out of control and get the better of you.

Be present

What you focus on is what you accomplish, and what you accomplish is what makes you successful.

If you're a successful leader, you may be invited to contribute to things that are outside of your organisation – perhaps to different boards, to industry committees, to workplace events, or to community groups. It's flattering to be asked to contribute to other organisations and to share your knowledge. This work may help to keep you motivated and expand your interests. However, if you take up additional opportunities, remember that you still need to be present for the organisation you lead. Don't run the risk of creating a leadership vacuum because you're off doing other things.

I once worked in an organisation where the CEO was incredibly successful. He started to expand his interests into different boards and industry groups. After a while, he started to be gone more often than he was at work. Other senior executives stepped up to fill the gap and made decisions they thought were in the best interests of the organisation. But the decisions they made weren't always in line with what the CEO wanted, and when he returned from his multiple absences he started to undo their decisions. It didn't take long for friction and conflict to emerge and for the CEO's effectiveness to drop.

Leading through intimidation

I worked for a guy in the Army once whom I can only describe as huge. He was solid muscle – probably weighing in at over

130 kg. And he was tall – somewhere around 195 cm. This guy liked to lead with intimidation.

I asked him about it once, and he openly admitted it to me. He said he'd been taught to lead people through intimidation, and he found it was effective. People always did what he wanted, but mostly because they were scared of him.

He wanted to know why I didn't seem intimidated by him. And the reason is that I don't consider physical size to be intimidating. There are much better ways to lead. I'm not particularly tall – only about 170 cm. But like this guy, I've got plenty of muscle. My brothers and my father are tall, and I'm used to being around big guys.

Physical size can be intimidating, but it shouldn't be. And just because it can be, that doesn't make it right. Physical intimidation or fear are not useful and sustainable ways to lead. One day, someone who is physically bigger or mentally stronger and more confident will come along. And if you haven't built a team based on loyalty and respect, that's when your leadership is going to go down.

A few years later, the intimidating guy was relieved of his duties. His leadership was toxic. He got things done all right, but he achieved them at the expense of his team.

Using external perspectives to locate the problem

I have had the pleasure of sitting on a number of boards and usually the board doesn't get closely involved in operational issues. However, sometimes we have to dip into the operational side of things to investigate when there seems to be a systemic problem or crisis.

In one instance the organisation whose board I was on was having problems delivering critical services and we needed to investigate why. At the board level, all we could see was that we had high staff turnover and difficulties keeping the service open. It's a service we're required to operate, but we were closing it several days per month because of our low staffing. It's also a service that requires highly skilled professionals who are not easy to recruit, particularly in a regional location.

Through our HR Director, we were able to understand that staff turnover was the problem. But as a board we needed to understand why the problem was occurring. We brought in an external consultant who discovered that the skilled staff in this service were reporting to someone who had been employed in the organisation for a very long time, but who had become toxic in the position. We needed an external consultant to get to the root of the problem because an internal investigation would have never uncovered it.

As a board, we couldn't get involved in addressing the issue. But we alerted the CEO to the source of the problem and made sure the CEO understood that our ability to deliver the service was being put at risk. Within months the service was beginning to turn around. The outlook of the team changed, and soon we found that staff retention had improved dramatically.

I understand that it must have been difficult for the CEO to be directed by the board to do something about the problem. I'm sure the CEO didn't want to have a difficult conversation. But in the interests of the welfare of the entire organisation and in the interests of our ability to deliver a required service, it had to be done.

Ten Top Principles for Leaders

1. People first
2. Add value to others
3. Never stop developing yourself
4. Be selfless
5. Be objective
6. Always be professional
7. Treat everyone with dignity and respect
8. Be consistent
9. Remove barriers
10. Be confident

1. People first

Leaders can only lead when people choose to follow them. That choice is important: people *choose* whether or not to follow you; you cannot successfully force them. You must always put your team and their needs at the forefront of your mind. They come first. Sometimes you'll need to perform a balancing act between what's best for your people and what's best for the organisation. Sometimes you'll need to make very difficult decisions. Always make the decision that's in the best interests of your people.

2. Add value to others

Add value by willingly sharing your knowledge and experience, helping others to develop their skills, and supporting people as they develop their own career. The more you work to develop your team, the more they will accomplish. You'll help them develop a higher sense of achievement, which will go a long way toward building confidence and retaining staff.

3. Never stop developing yourself

As a leader, you need to constantly update your leadership skills. There are two aspects to this. Firstly, change is the only constant in today's business environment. If you don't stay up to date with your industry and your operating environment, you will stagnate. What works for today's leaders may not work tomorrow. Secondly, there is always more to learn. Even if you study leadership every day for your entire life, you can never know all there is to know about leadership. If you continue to invest in your own learning, you will keep your skills fresh and relevant.

4. Be selfless

Your leadership is not about you. It's about your people. Never forget this. If you are looking for something that will build your ego, then leadership is not for you. A good leader gives away all the praise and accepts responsibility for everything that's bad.

5. Be objective

It's natural and very human to allow your personal feelings to influence your decision-making. However, your personal feelings must not guide your decisions. Do what you can to be objective, and you will make better decisions.

6. Always be professional

You are likely to find yourself in situations that are emotionally charged or in situations that present you with an ethical or moral dilemma. You can't let the situation get the better of you. Remember, at all times and in all situations, that you are a professional. Keep calm, no matter how stressed you may be. In stressful situations, others will look to you for guidance; you need to set a good example.

7. Treat everyone with dignity and respect

Everyone makes mistakes, and you will experience situations where someone has done something wrong – perhaps something that's not in line with the organisation's values or something that's illegal. Whatever happens, remind yourself that you must respond to the act and not to the person. Never treat someone badly because of what they have done. Remember the old saying 'take the high road' and always treat everyone with dignity and respect. Doing this will also help ensure you handle every situation with professionalism.

8. Be consistent

Always be consistent in your decision-making and your actions. Never leave your staff wondering which one of your many personalities they're dealing with. Your people need you to be dependable and predictable.

9. Remove barriers

As a leader, one of your primary responsibilities is to help your team to be as successful as possible. Often, they will encounter barriers to their success – perhaps a person, a process, a procedure, or a lack of resources. It's your job to address the barriers. You may need to have a difficult conversation with someone or redesign a process. Whatever the barrier is, you are the one with the authority to fix it.

10. Be confident

I'm sure you've heard the saying 'fake it till you make it'. Sometimes, that's what you'll need to do. There will be times when you may have no idea what to do or how to do it. You need enough confidence in yourself and your team to at least start. You need confidence in your ability to make decisions, learn, and adapt. With these, you'll discover there isn't much you can't handle. Things will not always be easy, but difficult situations will develop your leadership skills far more than business-as-usual. Remember that your people want a leader who is confident. Your confidence is contagious: the more confidence you show, the more confident your team will be, and the more they'll be settled when working through difficult times.

Make these your own

In this book I've outlined the way I think about leadership and explained some of the experiences that have informed my thinking. The ten leadership principles outlined above currently guide my work every day.

Leadership principles are dynamic. They need to develop and grow with you, as you gather experience, learn new insights, and refine your skills. They also need to respond to changing circumstances. While your underlying ethical and moral principles are unlikely to change, the leadership principles that are important in your everyday work will change over time.

If my leadership principles apply to you, then I encourage you to practise them, monitor your success in applying them, and learn from your experiences. As you develop more experience as a leader, develop your own set of leadership principles, tailored to the way you think and the work you do.

As leaders, we need to be nimble, flexible, motivated, and willing to learn. Truly good leaders never stop learning and never stop monitoring what's happening around them. They approach situations with a childlike enthusiasm and thirst for knowledge, ready to learn, think, adapt, and use insights to lead others.

Developing your leadership potential takes practice and time. The more you lead, and the more you think about what makes for successful leadership, the better you'll get.

Developing your leadership potential also takes discipline. You don't need to be the cleverest person in the room, or the most educated, or the most knowledgeable. What you do need to be is the one who shows up consistently, ready to take responsibility and accept uncertainty.

I wish you well on your leadership journey. I hope that my insights have provided you with some food for thought.

About the Author

Blake Repine spent more than 18 and a half years in various roles in the US Army before transitioning into the corporate world. He is a Senior Executive and Non-Executive Director with more than 20 years' experience in providing strategic vision, leadership and executive management. Blake has expertise in leadership and building strong, positive organisational cultures. He formulates strategies to drive improvement and innovation across a range of large and diverse organisations. Blake has facilitated growth within organisations by establishing targeted solutions and strategic plans to improve operational efficiency and leadership effectiveness.

As well as having attended multiple leadership courses in the Army, Blake also possesses a Bachelor of Science in Multidisciplinary Studies and a Master of Arts in Management and Leadership from Liberty University, an MBA from Norwich University and a Certificate of Completion in Disruptive Strategy from Harvard Business School. Blake is a Certified Professional with the Australian Human Resources Institute (AHRI) and a member of the Australian Institute of Company Director's (AICD).

Blake currently lives in Queensland, Australia with his wife and son. He is an avid weightlifter and a Level Three National Sport and Power Coach with the Australian Weightlifting Association. In his spare time, Blake also enjoys fishing, camping and riding motorcycles with his family.

www.ingramcontent.com/pod-product-compliance
Lightning Source LLC
Chambersburg PA
CBHW020325010526
44107CB00054B/1987